Confucianism

Ancient Philosophies

Created especially for students, this series of introductory books on the schools of ancient philosophy offers a clear yet rigorous presentation of core ideas. Designed to lay the foundation for a thorough understanding of their subjects, these fresh and engaging books are compact and reasonably priced, with illustrative texts in translation.

Published in the series:

1. *Stoicism*, by John Sellars

2. *Presocratics*, by James Warren

3. *Cynics*, by William Desmond

4. *Neoplatonism*, by Pauliina Remes

5. *Ancient Scepticism*, by Harald Thorsrud

6. *The Ancient Commentators on Plato and Aristotle*, by Miira Tuominen

7. *Epicureanism*, by Tim O'Keefe

8. *Plato*, by Andrew Mason

9. *Confucianism*, by Paul R. Goldin

Forthcoming in the series:

Classical Islamic Philosophy, by Deborah Black

Indian Buddhist Philosophy, by Amber Carpenter

The Sophists, by Richard McKirahan

Confucianism
Paul R. Goldin

University of California Press
Berkeley   Los Angeles

University of California Press, one of the most distinguished university presses in the United States, enriches lives around the world by advancing scholarship in the humanities, social sciences, and natural sciences. Its activities are supported by the UC Press Foundation and by philanthropic contributions from individuals and institutions. For more information, visit www.ucpress.edu.

For my students

University of California Press
Berkeley and Los Angeles, California

© 2011 Paul R. Goldin

Published simultaneously outside North America
by Acumen Publishing Limited.

ISBN   978-0-520-26969-9   (cloth : alk. paper)
ISBN   978-0-520-26970-5   (paper : alk. paper)

Library of Congress Control Number: 2010934246

Manufactured in the United Kingdom

19   18   17   16   15   14   13   12   11
10   9   8   7   6   5   4   3   2   1

The paper used in this publication meets the minimum requirements of

Contents

Chronology

618–906   Tang Dynasty
            768–824   *Han Yu*

907–60   Five Dynasties

960–1279   Song Dynasty
            1007–72   *Ouyang Xiu*
            1032–85   *Cheng Hao*
            1033–1107   *Cheng Yi*
            1130–1200   *Zhu Xi*

1271–1368   Yuan Dynasty

1368–1644   Ming Dynasty

1636–1912   Qing Dynasty

1912–49 (mainland)   Republic of China
1945– (Taiwan)
            1873–1929   *Liang Qichao*
            1879–1942   *Chen Duxiu*
            1893–1988   *Liang Shuming*

1949–   People's Republic of China

What Confucianism is and what Confucianism is not

Confucianism is China's oldest and most revered philosophy. In imperial times, Confucius's standing was so great that the few writers who questioned his teachings became notorious for that reason alone.[1] But in his own day, Confucius was taken as a wise but iconoclastic and potentially dangerous teacher of young men, and for many generations after his death, Confucians still struggled with exponents of other philosophies for primacy in the intellectual world of the so-called Warring States period (453–221 BCE). In keeping with the orientation of the Ancient Philosophies series, this book will focus on Confucianism as it was conceived and moulded by the earliest masters – in an age when Confucianism was regarded as but one of many viable philosophies, and did not yet enjoy the cultural supremacy that would come in later centuries. That later story will be reviewed briskly in the final chapter, along with a consideration of the standing of Confucianism today.

An exacting yet workable definition of Confucianism is crucial because the boundaries have been drawn both too broadly and too narrowly in the past. In this book, I shall use the term "Confucianism" to refer to the philosophy of Confucius (551–479 BCE), his disciples, and the numerous later thinkers who regarded themselves as followers of his tradition. This definition is restrictive enough to distinguish Confucianism from the many other philosophies and worldviews that flourished in traditional China, yet flexible enough to admit the literally hundreds of philosophers who considered themselves as his latter-day disciples. Like any vibrant and long-lived tradition, Confucianism was never a monolith and included, over time, a widening array of perspectives that often led to internal disagreement and debate. But competing Confucians rarely doubted each other's sincerity or commitment to applying the Master's teachings to the exigencies of their day. As we shall see, to be Confucian always meant to think for oneself. Any definition of Confucianism must be able to take this diversity into account.

At the same time, the contours of Confucianism are sometimes delineated so widely that it is misleadingly confused with traditional Chinese culture itself. This sort of conflation became especially common in the hands of revisionists in the nineteenth and twentieth centuries, who singled out virtually every objectionable feature of Chinese society as a vestige of the Confucian past. It is understandable that, in those miserable years, everything old and peculiar that differentiated China from the industrialized world was vilified, but the process of dismissing China's unique traditions as nothing more than Confucian detritus resulted in the inaccurate and unproductive conclusion that Confucianism was responsible for all of China's ills.[2]

Feminist writers, in this vein, have sometimes been too hasty in identifying all patriarchal structures in China with Confucianism.[3] Or consider the more limited example of footbinding, which brought unimaginable suffering to millions of women, but was in no way Confucian, as critics have often alleged. The original purpose of footbinding was to make women appear more sexually attractive by reducing the size of their feet and altering their gait; eventually, bound feet came to be so highly prized that mothers felt obliged to bind their own daughters' feet out of the conviction that no desirable man would ever marry them otherwise. Thus footbinding was, indeed, perpetuated within the patriarchal structure of the traditional Chinese family – but that is not the same thing as saying that the practice was Confucian. Confucianism sanctions actions and habits if and only if they are conducive to the cultivation of morality; making oneself more attractive for the marriage market would never have qualified as a sufficient concern. To be sure, moral meaning was occasionally attributed to footbinding, but only after the practice had already become widespread. For example, educated, upper-class women who had no choice but to continue to tend their bound feet (unbinding feet that have been bound since childhood is excruciatingly painful and does not, in any case, restore the physical integrity of the feet) reconceptualized this regimen as a manifestation of diligence, perseverance and other universally respected virtues. Similarly, male moralists sometimes opined that footbinding was beneficial in that it tended to keep women at home and off the streets (where they could only be courting trouble). In reality, however, ordinary women had no choice but to leave the home in order to get through the business of the day; their bound feet were merely an added physical burden.[4] Moreover, some of the most prominent devotees of footbinding were men who praised it for erotic, not moralistic, reasons: in this kind of literature, bound feet, hidden in their wrappings, are coy and titillating. Male connoisseurs adored the unique odour of dainty powder sprinkled over rotting flesh, while women, incapacitated by their bound feet, would supposedly become languorous and especially amenable to sex.[5]

One need not look to cases as extreme as that of footbinding to find misconceptions about Confucianism among sociologists and social historians. Too often one reads of "the Confucian family",[6] as though Confucianism prescribed a specific family structure. In fact, although Confucian texts have much to say about how people within a family should behave, they are surprisingly silent on the question of the ideal family structure (beyond the general assumption that every child will have a father and a mother). Canonical Confucian texts that seem to imply a certain family network – such as the *Odes* (*Shi* 詩), which include poetic narrations of rituals invoking lineage ancestors – refer to society in a period long before Confucius himself. Moreover, many different patterns of domestic organization have been attested through the millennia of Chinese history,[7] and it would be bizarre to declare that someone could not be recognized as a Confucian because he or she happened to be born into the wrong kind of family. What I think sociologists mean when they use phrases like "the Confucian family" (other than an invented tradition) is the extended family of the gentry who held sway in late imperial China. Modern films such as *Raise the Red Lantern* (*Da hong denglong gaogao gua* 大紅燈籠高高掛, 1991) have attempted to recreate the atmosphere of such clans. But the characteristics of gentry families have at least as much to do with issues of class, local politics and the apportioning of power as they do with Confucianism.[8]

The tendency to associate everything Chinese with Confucianism derives from the representation of China as a Confucian nation by Matteo Ricci (1552–1610) and his Jesuit confrères. Ricci was the first writer to introduce Chinese religion and philosophy to Western readers – earlier reporters, such as Marco Polo (*c.*1254–1324), had not discussed intellectual life to any substantive degree because they were unequipped to do so – and his status as Europe's arch-interpreter of China, combined with his unquestioned erudition, afforded him incalculable influence over the Western understanding of China.[9] (The very name "Confucius" comes from Jesuit missionaries; it is a Latinization of the Chinese term Kong fuzi 孔夫子, meaning roughly "revered Master Kong".) In a nutshell, Ricci's view was that Chinese culture was established by great sages like Confucius, who taught the same basic ethical principles that inform Christianity, even though they were not Christians because they could not have known of Christ. This contention was the justificatory cornerstone of Jesuit missionary practice (called "accommodationism"), which was to persuade Chinese audiences of the superiority of Christianity by providing a more compelling religious framework for China's own classics – rather than, like more radical missionaries, appraising their value as nil. Ricci was aware that not all Chinese were ardent Confucians, but explained away the other intellectual traditions (which he largely subsumed under the categories of Buddhism and idolatry) as accumulated dross that only obscured the original purity of Confucian teachings.[10] Without denying the privileged place of Confucian texts and doctrine in Chinese society, responsible historians must object to dispensing with everything else as mere pollution.

At the opposite hermeneutic extreme lie certain modern scholars who contend that the term "Confucianism" has no analytical value precisely because it has been deployed so profligately, and some, like Michael Nylan,[11] argue that the Chinese term *ru* 儒, which until recently has been translated as "Confucian" without too many misgivings, should be rendered as "classicist" instead. To take the second objection first: *ru* is undeniably the term that ancient Chinese speakers used when they wished to identify Confucius and his intellectual adherents. When the followers of Mo Di 墨翟 (d. *c.*390 BCE), an opponent of Confucianism who will figure into our discussion in later chapters, compiled a chapter entitled "Fei ru" 非儒, this clearly meant "Refuting the Confucians", not "Refuting the Classicists", inasmuch as each charge was directed specifically at Confucius or his disciples.[12] Moreover, interpreting *ru* as "classicist" would also seem to force Mo Di himself into the Ruist camp, because Mohists were no less devoted to the classics than Confucians were.[13] (The Mohist view was not that the canonical texts venerated by Confucians were invalid, but that Confucians horribly misinterpreted and misapplied them.) However they would have understood the term *ru*, Chinese audiences would never have thought that it included Mohists. Thus, although I would agree that it is sometimes inappropriate to restrict the sense of *ru* to "Confucians" (especially in later imperial contexts), the term nevertheless frequently refers to Confucius and people who explicitly identified themselves as followers of his teachings.[14]

And since there was such a body of thinkers – at best only loosely affiliated, and, as we shall see, by no means univocal – it is an overreaction to deny that "Confucianism" can be usefully employed as a designation of a certain philosophical orientation. All Confucians shared a set of basic convictions: (i) human beings are born with the capacity to develop morally; (ii) moral development begins with moral self-cultivation, that is, reflection on one's own behaviour and concerted improvement where it is found lacking; (iii) by perfecting oneself in this manner, one also contributes to the project of perfecting the world; (iv) there were people in the past who perfected themselves, and then presided over an unsurpassably harmonious society – these people are called "sages" (*sheng* 聖 or *shengren* 聖人). Not all Confucians agreed about what moral self-cultivation entails, or how we should go about it, but all accepted that we can and must do it, and that it is a task of utmost urgency.

The following chapters will focus on the three most influential ancient Confucians, namely Confucius (Kong Qiu 孔丘, 551–479 BCE), Mencius (Meng Ke 孟軻, 371–289 BCE) and Xunzi 荀子 (Master Xun, or Xun Kuang 荀況, c.310–c.210 BCE). In addition, three anonymous texts will be considered: *Great Learning* (*Daxue* 大學) and *Canon of Filial Piety* (*Xiaojing* 孝經), which are accorded their own brief section, as well as *Application of Equilibrium* (*Zhongyong* 中庸), which is cited at appropriate junctures. This selection does not cover all the ancient material that can be reasonably associated with Confucianism,[15] but it is the core.

ONE

Confucius and his disciples

The Master said: "People can enlarge the Way. It is not that
the Way can enlarge people." (*Analects* 15.28)[1]

Confucius is the most influential thinker in Chinese civilization
and the first whose philosophy can be reconstructed to any significant degree. In China, he has been known by many posthumous
names and titles, the most revealing being *xianshi* 先師, which can
be understood as both "the teacher from the past" and "the foremost
teacher". For Confucius was, as far as we can tell, the first teacher of
his kind and the inaugurator of one of the most glorious philosophical ages of any ancient culture.

Confucius was a ritual master, and there were surely many ritual
masters in the generations preceding him. Museum-goers know
that, in the bounteous Chinese Bronze Age, kings and elite lineages
produced untold numbers of bronze vessels in various typical forms
with precise ritual functions.[2] It is clear from assemblages in burials
that each type of vessel was necessary for the full concert of rituals, and archaic literature – including the many inscriptions cast on
these bronze vessels – tells us that the correct performance of these
rites was crucial to securing the blessing of the spirits. Deceased
ancestors were thought to perdure after death as spirits who had
to be properly cultivated with sacrifices and other ritual obsequies.

As early as the Shang 商 dynasty (*c*.1600–*c*.1045 BCE), for example, kings would divine about the source of their toothaches; for only after it was determined which ancestral spirit was responsible for the affliction could the appropriate steps be taken to placate him or her. (Ancestresses were no less terrifying in this respect than ancestors.) And the toothache was understood as a warning to rectify whatever wrongdoing or oversight had irked the spirit in question. Toothache today – flood or earthquake or some comparable catastrophe tomorrow.[3]

Doubtless, then, the ritual culture implied by the numerous surviving bronze artefacts required ritual masters who could explain to new generations how each vessel was to be used. And there are hints in ancient texts that some of these ritual masters began to incorporate moral principles into their curriculum: it was not enough simply to carry out the appropriate sacrifice correctly; it was necessary also to live up to the right moral standard. What these high ancients really said, however, is for the most part beyond recovery, as there are only the scantest records of their utterances. Confucius was apparently the first to have his teachings documented by his disciples, and, not coincidentally, seems to have emphasized the moral aspect of correct ritual practice to an unprecedented degree. Thus he transformed the ancient role of ritual master, expert in the ways of cauldrons and platters, into something that we would call a moral philosopher.

The prime difficulty facing any modern reader of Confucius, however, is that he did not leave behind any written work. Tradition has ascribed to him the redaction of certain canonical texts, such as the *Springs and Autumns* (*Chunqiu* 春秋) and *Changes of Zhou* (*Zhouyi* 周易), but the attribution is not fully convincing, and in any case no one suggests that he *composed* these texts – only that he arranged pre-existing material in a morally revealing way. There are dozens of sources that record this or that saying as having been uttered by Confucius, the most authoritative of which is the so-called *Analects* (*Lunyu* 論語), but these were all produced after his death.

There are two main reasons why Confucius never felt compelled to leave behind a treatise or similar written text. First, in his day, writing was not the most important means of communication. In our world, for the past several centuries, the surest way to publish one's ideas has been to put them in writing, and even as today's technology has created useful media besides the old-fashioned book, writing is unlikely to disappear soon – as ubiquitous texting and blogging attest. But Confucius's society was small enough that oral communication sufficed for many more purposes than we might assume. When a wise man advised a king, he would typically say, "Your servant has *heard* …", not "Your servant has *read* …" Any idea worth repeating would be transmitted from one mouth to the next. And as soon as people stopped repeating it, it died. To be sure, writing had already been known for a good millennium by Confucius's time, but its uses seem to have been mostly hieratic.[4] If you needed to communicate with ancestral spirits, you needed a scribe. But if you wished to discuss right conduct with your neighbour, you just started talking. Thus one reason why Confucius never wrote down his teachings is that he never imagined it would be necessary to do so. His legacy would continue through his disciples, who would pass it on – orally – to disciples of their own.

Second, Confucius may have deemed writing incompatible with one of his most important ideas: that people need to think for themselves. "I begin with one corner", he said; "if [a student] cannot return with the other three corners, I do not repeat myself" (*Analects* 7.8). A teacher can be expected to lay down the guidelines, but students must then fill out the rest of the picture on their own.[5] Throughout the *Analects*, Confucius is shown to be uneasy about affirming any universal principle; rightness and wrongness must be judged anew in every situation. Thus, in teaching, it is a mistake merely to deliver insensate lectures to audiences of students with disparate needs:

> Zilu 子路 [i.e. Zhong Yóu 仲由, 542–480 BCE] asked: "Should one practise something after having heard it?"
> The Master said: "You have a father and elder brother who are still alive; how would you practise something after having heard it?"

Ran Yŏu 冉有 [b. 522 BCE] asked: "Should one practise something after having heard it?"

The Master said: "One should practise something after having heard it."

Gongxi Hua 公西華 [i.e. Gongxi Chi 公西赤, b. 539 BCE] said: "When Yóu [i.e. Zilu] asked whether one should practise something after having heard it, you said: 'Your father and elder brother are still alive.' When Qiu [i.e. Ran Yŏu] asked whether one should practise something after having heard it, you said: 'One should practise something after having heard it.' I am confused, and venture to ask about this".

The Master said: "Qiu is withdrawn; thus I urged him forward. Yóu [has the eagerness] of two men; thus I held him back." 　　　　　　　　　　　　　　　　(*Analects* 11.22)

This exchange is included in the *Analects* for the insight that two different students should not necessarily be taught the same lesson. But in a *written* document, to be read by strangers not in his presence (or indeed after his death), it would have been impossible for Confucius to tailor his teachings in this manner. Even with the best of intentions, his philosophy might then have become what he despised most: an authority telling you what is right in all times and places. Writing fixes statements, and Confucius wished his statements to remain fluid. (It is rather like the difference between hearing a great musician in a live performance, where there can be inexhaustible variation, and hearing him or her through a recording, which is the same no matter how many times you play it.)

For this reason, Confucius also avoided full expositions of his thinking. Western philosophers may be disappointed to see no sustained treatises, no tight syllogisms in his work. Rather, Confucian rhetoric typically uses allusive language – often invoking nature and sometimes reaching a level of discourse that can only be considered poetic – in order to spur students to think through the morals on their own. For example: "The Master said: 'Only after the year has grown cold does one know that the pine and cypress are the last to wither'" (*Analects* 9.27).

A memorable meiosis – for pines and cypresses are not merely the last to wither; they almost *never* wither. As anyone in Confucius's society would have known from daily exposure to the living world, pines and cypresses not only remain green throughout the year, but also are among the longest-lived trees on earth. Usually *Analects* 9.27 is understood as a comment on friendship: fair-weather friends may, like beautiful plum or cherry blossoms, seem attractive in times of abundance, but true friends resemble evergreens, maintaining their colour in all seasons of the year. But it is also, on a deeper level, a statement about the usefulness of looking to patterns in nature as a guide through the perplexities of life, as well as a reminder that the value of things cannot be gauged by their momentary appeal. At the same time, it is an assertion of the need for experience, and not just reason, in judgement: for if the character of pines and cypresses cannot be appreciated before the year has grown cold, then someone who has never experienced winter cannot possibly comprehend how they surpass the gaudy blooms of springtime. Thus it is not surprising that names bearing the word *song* 松, "pine", were favoured by literati in traditional China,[6] and the hardy pine – often shown gnarled and twisted in snowy landscapes – was a mainstay of Chinese nature painting.[7]

After Confucius's death, his disciples knew that they had lost an icon, and resolved to select for posterity's benefit the most important sayings and exchanges that they could remember from their encounters with the Master. This is, at any rate, the traditional story behind the text known as *Analects*, whose Chinese title, *Lunyu*, means "selected" (*lun*) "sayings" (*yu*). There are various scholarly theories about the provenance of the received text by that name, which contains twenty chapters and has come to be regarded as the most respected of several repositories of sayings attributed to Confucius. One unavoidable difficulty is that it seems to be unattested before the Han 漢 dynasty (206 BCE–220 CE).[8] But the language is demonstrably older than Han-dynasty language,[9] and it is possible to reconstruct a coherent philosophy from its core chapters; therefore, like most (but not all)[10] scholars, I accept the first fifteen chapters as the closest we can come today to reading Confucius's own words.

(Chapters 16–20, as has been observed for centuries, are written in a more expansive style and probably contain additions from later times;[11] consequently, they will be cited below only when their testimony can be corroborated by passages in Chapters 1–15.) There are many other early texts that attribute sayings to Confucius, but it is always necessary to interpret these critically. The *Zhuangzi* 莊子, for example, which imparts a philosophy uncompromisingly opposed to that of Confucius, shows him saying all sorts of embarrassing and self-demeaning things, and it would be a mistake to put the same stock in such quotations as in the *Analects* or other material endorsed by Confucian disciples.[12]

Of his life and heritage we know only the barest of details,[13] which eager hands eventually embellished incredibly. Within a few centuries, Confucius was depicted as a demigod with supernatural bodily features and superhuman physical strength.[14] In reality, his ancestry was murky;[15] his father, called Shuliang He 叔梁紇 in most sources, may have been a warrior from a place called Zou 陬/鄒; Confucius may have been conceived outdoors; he may have served his home state of Lu 魯 in a minor capacity (Minister of Justice, *sikou* 司寇, according to tradition); he travelled to several states offering his counsel and had audiences with multiple feudal lords; he attracted dozens of disciples, some of whom were among the most influential young men in his community; he probably died at an age above 70. Confucius's importance lies not in the details of his life, but in the philosophy that he left behind.

* * *

A modern reader of Confucius, then, is faced with this task: using the *Analects* and perhaps a handful of other early texts, none of which was written by Confucius himself, to reconstruct the philosophy of a master who would have preferred to teach you personally. Fortunately, careful reading of the *Analects* reveals a unique and consistent philosophical attitude. Confucius himself insists on several occasions that although his teachings may appear disparate, there is "one thing with which to string [everything] together" (*yi yi guan zhi* 一以貫之).

For modern readers, it is probably best to begin a survey of his philosophy with his views of spirits and the afterlife. He was principially agnostic:

> The Master was critically ill. Zilu asked leave to pray. The Master said: "Is there such a thing?"
> Zilu responded: "There is. The eulogy says: 'We pray for you above and below to the spirits of the upper and lower worlds.'"
> The Master said: "My prayer is of long standing."
>
> (*Analects* 7.34)

Notice that Confucius does not go so far as to deny the potential value of prayer; he only questions it, and concludes with the unforgettable instruction that, if it has any value at all, prayer consists not of formulas repeated mechanically from predetermined liturgies, but in one's everyday words and deeds. Throughout the *Analects*, we see Confucius deconstructing received religion, and enjoining his disciples to think through an entirely new moral system with *human interaction* as its base,[16] not veneration of ghosts and spirits: "Fan Chi 樊遲 [b. 515 BCE] asked about wisdom. The Master said: 'To take what is due to the people as one's duty, and to revere the ghosts and spirits, but keep them at a distance, can be called wisdom'" (*Analects* 6.20). The most famous phrase from this exchange, "revere the ghosts and spirits, but keep them at a distance" (*jing guishen er yuan zhi* 敬鬼神而遠之), is endlessly repeated, but the first half of Confucius's response to Fan Chi is no less important. If you are looking for moral bedrock, find it in obligations to other people mandated by your relations with them. But what exactly is "what is due to the people"? You have to determine this for yourself. And above all do what you think is right, not what you think the ghosts and spirits want you to do. For we can never really know what the ghosts and spirits want anyway (at least not until we become ghosts and spirits ourselves).

Confucius is not an atheist – he concedes that there are ghosts and spirits,[17] and that it is advisable not to offend them – but he believes that pondering the afterlife and the supernatural will impede moral reasoning:

> Jilu [i.e. Zilu] asked about the services for ghosts and spirits. The Master said: "You do not yet know how to serve people. How will you be able to serve ghosts?"
> "May I be so bold as to ask about death?"
> [Confucius] said: "You do not yet know life. How can you know death?" (*Analects* 11.11)

One last passage in the same vein comes from Chapter 17, in other words one of the spurious chapters, but is worth citing here because it anticipates a crucial theme in later Confucianism: we may not be able to read the will of the gods, but we can infer how nature works by observing it. Nature abides by regular and discernible patterns, which we can learn by intelligent observation and then apply to our own lives:

> The Master said: "I wish to be without speech."
> Zigong 子貢 [i.e. Duanmu Ci 端木賜, 520–456 BCE] said: "If you do not speak, then what will we, your children, have to transmit from you?"
> The Master said: "What does Heaven say? The four seasons progress by it; the many creatures are born by it. What does Heaven say?" (*Analects* 17.19)

So much for traditional religion; while most other people in Confucius's day were trying to find their moral bearings by worshipping gods and spirits, and attempting to ascertain their mysterious wishes through divination and other questionable ceremonies, Confucius told his students to set aside that credulous mode and focus instead on human relationships in the world of the living. And how do we treat other human beings? This is where the "one thing with which to string everything together" comes into play. First, the best-known passage, in which Confucius addresses his student, Zeng Can 曾參 (505–436 BCE?):

> The Master said: "Can! In my Way, there is one thing with which to string [everything] together."
>
> Master Zeng said: "Yes."
>
> The Master went out, and the disciples asked: "What was he referring to?"
>
> Master Zeng said: "The Way of the Master is nothing other than *zhong* 忠 and *shu* 恕." (*Analects* 4.15)

Zhong and *shu* are difficult terms that need to be unpacked by referring to Confucius's own usage in other passages, as they have acquired other distracting senses in ordinary Chinese. *Zhong*, for instance, is usually understood today as "loyalty", but that is not even close to what Confucius meant. *Shu* is the more consequential of the two.[18] Remember that Confucius said there was *one thing* in his Way, and yet Master Zeng explained it to the other disciples as *zhong* and *shu* – two things. In two very similar passages, but this time with Zigong as the interlocutor, Confucius implies that the one thing is not *zhong* and *shu*, but merely *shu*. At the same time, he gives a direct definition:

> Confucius said: "Ci, do you consider me one who knows things by having studied much?"
>
> [Zigong] replied: "Yes. Is that not so?"
>
> [Confucius] said: "It is not so. I have one thing with which to string everything together." (*Analects* 15.2)

> Zigong asked: "Is there one word that one can practise throughout one's life?"
>
> That Master said: "Is it not *shu* [reciprocity]? What you yourself do not desire, do not do to others."(*Analects* 15.23)

"What you yourself do not desire, do not do to others" (*ji suo bu yu, wu shi yu ren* 己所不欲, 勿施於人) is the cornerstone of Confucian ethics (and its similarity to the Golden Rule is one of the features of Confucianism that inspired Ricci), but for modern readers an immediate qualification is necessary: in practice, *shu* has to be interpreted as doing unto others as you would have others do unto you *if you had the same social role as they*.[19] Otherwise, *shu* would require fathers to treat their sons in the same manner that their sons treat them – a practice that no Confucian has ever considered appropriate.

The detail that the calculus of *shu* requires us also to take the actors' social status into account may not be clear from the *Analects*, but is unmistakable in another famous statement attributed to Confucius and recorded in the *Application of Equilibrium* (*Zhongyong* 中庸):

> *Zhong* and *shu* are not far from the Way. What you would not suffer others to do to you, do not do to them. There are four things in the Way of the Noble Man, none of which I have been able to do. I have not been able to serve my father as I demand of my son. I have not been able to serve my lord as I demand of my servant. I have not been able to serve my elder brother as I demand of my younger brother. I have not been able to do unto my friends first as I demand of them. (*Zhongyong* 13)

To revisit the example of a father and son: in order to apply *shu* correctly, the question for a son to consider is not how his father treats him, but how he would like his own son to treat him. *Shu* is a relation not between two individuated people, but between two social roles. How does one treat one's father? In the same way that one would want to be treated by one's son *if one were a father oneself*.[20]

There are well-known difficulties, not addressed by Confucius in the *Analects*, with ethical systems based on the notion of reciprocity. The most important is the objection that different people can sincerely wish to be treated in different ways, and, as a result, might treat other people in different ways too – without necessarily being wicked or hypocritical.[21] Confucius's silence on this problem is significant. Either he believes the people will always come to the same general conclusions about how they wish to be treated (if they practise *shu* without self-delusion), or he believes that such varying interpretations of the demands of *shu* are permissible as long as people's actions rest on a legitimate basis of moral reasoning. In the past I have leaned more towards the former interpretation (implicitly attributing to Confucius a somewhat rigid conception of human nature), but now I favour the latter. Enslaving others under the pretext that it would be best for slaves to be enslaved would never be acceptable as *shu*. But if we observe a crime while it is being committed and can do something about it, is it better to call the police or intervene personally? Either option would be praiseworthy if we truly believed that it is what would be most helpful. Only the person who does nothing at all would be open to condemnation.

Shu is crucial to Confucian ethics, as we shall see presently, but before going on we must ask what is meant by *zhong*. Confucius never defines *zhong* as helpfully as he defines *shu*, and some questionable modern interpretations of *zhong* are based on the Neo-Confucian understanding of *zhong* as "making the most of oneself" (*jinji* 盡己). Thus D. C. Lau, for example, has rendered *zhong* too diffusely as "doing one's best".[22] In my view, *zhong* has an effective meaning of "being honest with oneself in dealing with others"[23] in the *Analects*, and the key passage is, not coincidentally, placed in the mouth of the same Master Zeng:

> Master Zeng said: "Everyday I examine myself on three counts. In planning on behalf of others, have I failed to be *zhong*? In associating with friends, have I failed to be trustworthy? Have I transmitted anything that I do not practise habitually?" (*Analects* 1.4)

What Master Zeng means by the first of his three tests is whether, in carrying out *shu*, he has done wrong by others by pretending that what is beneficial to *himself* is what *they* would want him to do. *Shu* is instantly perverted if it is applied dishonestly, but self-deception is not always easy to discover and root out if one does not vigilantly review one's own actions. For this reason, *zhong* is frequently paired with *xin* 信, "trustworthiness", in the *Analects* (as in 1.8: "Esteem *zhong* and trustworthiness").

To return to *shu*. Confucius's identification of *shu* as "What you yourself do not desire, do not do to others" helps explain several other passages in the *Analects*. Confucius's disciples knew that although he spoke of several different virtues, the most important was called *ren* 仁, "humanity". (The word is homophonous with *ren* 人, "human being", and Confucians have been fond of taking advantage of this aural connection.)[24] "The Master said: 'The wise take joy in rivers; the humane take joy in mountains. The wise are active; the humane are still. The wise are joyous; the humane are long-lived'" (*Analects* 6.24). Clearly both the wise and the humane are praised in this statement, but a listener attuned to Confucius's suggestive style will recognize that, in this formulation, humanity comes before wisdom in the same way that rivers flow down from mountains. Rivers always move; mountains remain stationary till the end of time. There can be mountains without rivers, but no rivers without mountains.

It must have been frustrating to some of Confucius's disciples that he never defined *ren*; he always talked around it (using metaphors involving mountains and rivers), as he preferred to spur his students to come to their own understanding of it. Thus one finds examples where a disciple will come to Confucius with some overblown statement, and ask whether this would qualify as *ren*:

> Zigong said: "Suppose there is someone who extensively confers benefits on the people and was able to help the multitude. What about that – can one call this humanity?"
> The Master said: "Why make an issue of humanity? Would this not have to be sagehood? Could even [the sage kings] Yao 堯 and Shun 舜 find infirmity in someone [like that]? Now as for humanity – what one wishes to establish in oneself one establishes in others; what one wishes to advance in oneself, one advances in others. The ability to take what is near as an analogy can be called the method of humanity." (*Analects* 6.28)

In other words, Zigong's standard is impossibly high: only sages – whom ordinary people cannot ever hope to match – could ever do as much as Zigong demands. Humanity is something much simpler: it is the virtue based on the method of *shu*. If we work tirelessly to make *shu* our regular practice, we will be on the path of humanity itself. *Shu* is placing oneself in the position of others, and acting towards them as one imagines they would desire. How can one possibly imagine what someone else would desire? By taking oneself as an analogy.

The definition of *shu* as not doing to others what you yourself do not desire also unlocks an otherwise enigmatic exchange:

> Zigong said: "What I do not desire others to do to me, I do not desire to do to them."
> The Master said: "Ci, you have not attained to that."
> *(Analects* 5.11)

The Master bursts Zigong's self-satisfied bubble. Zigong has obviously heard Confucius define *shu* and emphasize its significance (perhaps in the same dialogue recorded in *Analects* 6.28), and wishes to impress his master by asserting that he will adopt the same principle. Confucius responds that it is more easily said that done. Practising *shu* is not a matter of making grand announcements, but doing it one's whole life. ("My prayer is of long standing", as Confucius said.)

Confucius has much more to say about *ren*, and links it to the concept of *li* 禮, "ritual", in a dense and easily misunderstood passage:

> Yan Yuan 顏淵 [i.e. Yan Hui 顏回, 521–481? BCE] asked about humanity. The Master said: "Overcome the self and return to ritual in order to practise humanity. If you can overcome the self and return to ritual for one day, the world will bring humanity home to you. Does the practice of humanity emerge from the self, or does it arise from others?"[25]
> Yan Yuan said: "May I ask for an overview?"
> The Master said: "Do not look in opposition to the rites. Do not listen in opposition to the rites. Do not speak in opposition to the rites. Do not move in opposition to the rites."

Yan Yuan said: "Although I am not clever, I ask leave to make this saying my business."   (*Analects* 12.1)

Western interpreters of Confucius have frequently mischaracterized *li* as something like a code of conduct,[26] leading to serious misconceptions about what Confucius means by not looking, listening, speaking, or moving in opposition to the rites. One might think there is a discrete and knowable code, called *li*, that one can rely on for guidance in all matters: if you do not know how to act, cleave to the *li*, and you will never be wrong. This might also have been the standard conception of *li* in Confucius's own day: a practicable code that ambitious young men hoped to learn from experienced ritual masters. The problem is that this understanding of *li* is inadequate for Confucius, because he explicitly *contrasts* the rites with anything like a predetermined code (and, to this extent, the very translation of *li* as "rite" or "ritual" can be misleading):

The Master said: "If you guide them with legislation, and unify them with punishments, then the people will avoid [the punishments] but have no conscience. If you guide them with virtue, and unify them with ritual, then they will have a conscience; moreover, they will correct themselves."   (*Analects* 2.3)

Legislation and punishments are not ineffective; on the contrary, they are highly effective, because they make people do whatever is necessary to avoid being punished. But what laws and punishments cannot do is effect any moral transformation in the populace, and this is (as will soon become clear) the only legitimate purpose of government. Laws and punishments are like traffic lights at an intersection. Traffic lights are effective at preventing accidents because most people abide by them. And why do they abide by them? For two obvious reasons: they do not want to be fined for going through a red light, and they do not want to cause an accident by driving headlong into traffic. (The former would seem to be the overriding concern, as most motorists stop at red lights even in the middle of the night, when the intersection is empty.) Confucius's point would be that traffic lights do not make anyone a better person. One can be a perfectly wicked person and still stop unfailingly at every red light. Traffic lights simply mould our conduct, not our inner morality. And this, as far as Confucius is concerned, is not enough; what government really needs are not laws and punishments, but virtue and ritual. Only virtue and ritual can aid in moral self-cultivation.

Thus, as tempting as the interpretation may be, *li* cannot refer to a code of conduct, and therefore in order to understand *Analects* 12.1 – "Do not look in opposition to the rites; do not listen in opposition to the rites; do not speak in opposition to the rites; do not move in opposition to the rites" – we need to reconstruct the meaning of *li* by examining its usage elsewhere in the text.

The most revealing passage has to do with rituals in a ceremonial hall:

> The Master said: "A cap of hemp [is prescribed by] the rites, but today [one uses] jet-black silk. This is frugal, and I follow the majority. To bow at the bottom of the hall [is prescribed by] the rites, but today one bows at the top [of the hall]. This is self-aggrandizing, so I oppose the majority; I follow [the tradition of bowing at] the bottom [of the hall]."
>
> (*Analects* 9.3)

In Confucius's day, the ritual cap of hemp was considered more extravagant than one of silk (which was a plentiful material). The passage addresses the question of when it is and is not permissible to alter the received rituals. Substituting a more frugal ceremonial hat for the fancy one prescribed by the rites is acceptable, but bowing at the top of the hall instead of the bottom of the hall is not. It follows, then, that the rites are subject to emendation in practice, but one cannot depart from them capriciously or groundlessly. Rather, they must be practised in such a way as to convey and reinforce deeper moral principles. Nor can one simply follow the majority. Laudable practice of the rites requires thinking for oneself.

Li is best understood, then, as embodied virtue, the thoughtful somatic expression of basic moral principles, without which the ceremonies are void. A disciple named Zixia 子夏 (i.e. Bu Shang 卜商, b. 507 BCE) seems to be indicating this point in his subtle analysis of a classical poetic verse:

> Zixia asked: "'Oh, her artful smile is dimpled. Oh, her beautiful eye is black-and-white. Oh, a plain [background] on which to apply the highlights.'[27] What does this refer to?"
> The Master said: "In painting, everything follows the plain [background]".
> [Zixia] said: "Does ritual follow [in similar fashion]?"
> The Master said: "Shang, it is you who have inspired me. Finally I have someone to discuss the *Odes* with."
> *(Analects* 3.8)

Confucius's fascination with the canonical *Odes* is evident throughout the *Analects*. On one occasion (*Analects* 16.13), he is said to have told his son that if he does not study the *Odes*, he will have "nothing with which to speak" (*wu yi yan* 無以言). All early Confucians joined him in regarding the *Odes* as the supreme model of dignified expression.[28] In this particular passage, Zixia presumably means to say that the rituals, significant though they may be, are effective only if practised by those who have morally prepared themselves for the task. Someone who is morally alive, then, must reassess at every moment how best to perform the rites. The rites prescribe a fine hat? Ah, but a plain one would be more frugal. Choose a plain one. The majority bows at the top of the hall even though the rites call for bowing at the bottom of the hall? Bowing at the top of the hall is self-aggrandizing, and that sends the wrong message, even if it has become customary. Bow at the bottom of the hall instead. Far from a static code of conduct, *li* is the sum total of all the moral calculations that a thinking Confucian must go through before acting. *Li* is in constant flux; it must be constantly reinterpreted and reapplied to suit changing situations.

Thus when Confucius tells Yan Yuan not to look, listen, speak or move in opposition to the rites, he does not mean that Yan Yuan need only memorize a certain body of accepted conventions and take care always to follow them; rather, using the fuller sense of *li*, he means that Yan Yuan must ask himself how to put the most humane face on the rites in each new situation, and then to carry them out conscientiously. What sounds like a deceptively simple instruction is really a demand that Yan Yuan not only act with unflagging moral awareness but also assess *for himself* the right course of action at every moment.[29]

* * *

Confucius's statement that only virtue and ritual satisfy the moral demands of government opens the door to the next major theme in his philosophy. The core passage is *Analects* 12.17: "Ji Kangzi 季康子 [i.e. Jisun Fei 季孫肥, d. 468 BCE] asked Confucius about government. Confucius answered: 'To govern is to correct. If you lead with rectitude, who will dare not be correct?'" "To govern is to correct" is a keen paronomasia in Chinese, for the word for "government" (*zheng* 政) is a homophonous derivative of the word for "correction" or "rectitude" (*zheng* 正).[30] While our most prominent political metaphor in the West is the ship of state – the word "governor" originally refers to a steersman, after all – Confucius's metaphor is that government is a project of moral correction. In his pithy response to Ji Kangzi, he makes two fundamental claims: government is inescapably a moral endeavour, and the ruler's behaviour has an irresistible influence on his subjects. Confucius returns to these points repeatedly: "The Master said: 'If he himself is rectified, [his will] is carried out even if he does not command it; if he himself is not rectified, [his will] is not followed even if he does command it'" (*Analects* 13.6).

The ruler's verbal commands, then, are essentially pleonastic: the people will examine his conduct, and adjust their own accordingly. Government is not successful if those at the top abuse their position in order to gratify their desires. If the people see that their ruler is greedy, they will become thievish themselves, but if they see that he has learned how to restrain his desires, they will emulate him in this respect as well. "Ji Kangzi was concerned about thievery, and asked Confucius about it. Confucius responded: 'If you were not covetous, they would not steal even if you were to reward them for it'" (*Analects* 12.18). And immediately another response to the same Ji Kangzi, who now proposes to execute all those who act immorally, eliciting a line that has been treasured for centuries:

> Confucius responded: "In exercising government, why do you need to kill? If you desire goodness, the people will be good. The character of the noble man is like wind; the character of the petty man is like grass. When the wind [blows] over the grass, it must bend." (*Analects* 12.19)

The people will sway in whichever direction their superiors incline them.

Rulers have this power to shape the people's conduct because of another fundamental belief of Confucius: *all* human conduct affects every other person near the actor. Morality spreads: "The virtuous are not orphans; they will have neighbours" (*Analects* 4.25). Indeed, people whom we might consider barbaric are uncultivated only because they have not yet had the benefit of moral guidance. In the presence of the right teacher, they could not help becoming rectified themselves:

> The Master wished to dwell among the several barbarians. Someone said: "They are rude; how will you get along?"
>
> The Master said: "If a noble man dwelled there, what rudeness would there be?" (*Analects* 9.13)

Everyone has a stake in the moral standing of the human community, and at the same time the wherewithal to affect it either positively or negatively. But rulers are uniquely positioned, because of their unparalleled authority, to affect whole nations. A scrupulous gentleman might be able to affect his family and perhaps a few of his neighbours; a sage ruler, by contrast, could conceivably lead all human beings to that ideal Confucian kingdom of universal moral excellence. And with great power comes great responsibility: while a selfish commoner will probably never be more than a local pest, a tyrant could hurl his whole kingdom to perdition. Most rulers, in

Confucius's view, do not comprehend the momentous duties that accompany their lofty titles.

A question about politics occasioned yet another famous remark:

> Lord Jing of Qi 齊景公 [r. 547–490 BCE] asked Confucius about government. Confucius answered: "The lord acts as a lord, the minister as a minister, the father as a father, the son as a son."
> The lord said: "Excellent! Surely, if the lord does not act as a lord, nor the minister as a minister, nor the father as a father, nor the son as a son, then although I might have grain, would I be able to eat it?" (*Analects* 12.11)

Many modern readers are puzzled by this exchange, not least because Lord Jing's enthusiastic agreement does not seem to shed much further light on Confucius's pithy saying. (The main reason for Lord Jing's presence in the passage is probably to show that Confucius was sought out by some of the loftiest men in the Chinese world for his opinions on government; today's equivalent would be something like "Vice President Biden asked Professor So-and-so about healthcare reform".)

"The lord acts as a lord, the minister as a minister, the father as a father, the son as a son" is beautifully terse in Chinese (*jun jun chen chen fu fu zi zi* 君君臣臣父父子子), because the pliable grammar of the classical language allows any word to function as any part of speech depending on its place in the sentence. Thus *jun jun* means "the lord" (*jun*, noun) "acts as a lord" (*jun*, verb). The saying could conceivably be read as an apology for pre-existing power relations – if you are not the lord, you must hold your tongue, because only the lord can be the lord – but this is not how Confucius's words were understood by the tradition. Rather, "to act as a lord", "to act as a minister", "to act as a father" and "to act as a son" are taken to be moral demands: if a ruler, minister, father or son are to be reckoned as such, they must act as required by their positions in society. "To act as a lord" means to live up to the moral demands of the position of rulership that we have outlined above. It means to be vigilant about one's own conduct so as to provide a worthy model for the people to follow in their quest for moral self-cultivation.

"To act as a lord" naturally does not mean to enforce one's will imperiously and disregard the upright remonstrance of concerned ministers. That would be "to act *not* as a lord", and indeed lords who act in such a heedless way do not deserve to be called "lords" at all.[31] Confucius's statement is one of the oldest examples of a typical theme in early Chinese philosophy: rectifying names (*zhengming* 正名),[32] or making sure that names fit the realities they are supposed to represent. In Confucius's formulation, rectifying names is fundamentally a moral undertaking: appropriate names and titles are determined by the moral standing of the people who bear them.[33] A lord is someone who acts like a lord; a tyrant is someone who acts like a tyrant. In the same fashion, Confucius redefined the old title *junzi* 君子, meaning literally "son of a lord" and denoting a member of the hereditary aristocracy, in moral terms: a *junzi* is someone who acts as a *junzi* should, regardless of his or her birth.[34] Defenders of the entrenched social hierarchy would thus not have been enthusiastic Confucians. (Throughout this book, *junzi* in this moral sense is rendered as "noble man".)

Confucius's recipe for good government permits some other inferences. First, modern readers can hardly avoid observing that all four characters – the lord, the minister, the father and the son – are male. It was a social reality in Confucius's day that lords and ministers were without exception male, but instead of "the father" and "the son", he might well have said "fathers and mothers" and "sons and daughters". Readers must decide for themselves how much to make of this problem. On the one hand, there is little reason why Confucius's ideas could not be extended today to include women as well;[35] on the other hand, there is also little reason to suppose that he himself would have thought to do so. All his disciples were male, and his few comments about women suggest that he thought most consequential actions were undertaken by men.[36]

Another inescapable observation is that the four cardinal roles are all relative. No one can be a lord without a minister, a minister without a lord, a father without a son, or a son without a father. By the same token, it is possible for the same person to play more than one of these roles in different situations and in relation to different people. All males are sons, and thus any father is not only a father to his son but also a son to his own father. Similarly, a minister may be a lord in his own right, but a minister to a lord higher than he; indeed, in Bronze Age politics, even the highest king, the Son of Heaven, is conceived as a lord to all other human beings but only a vicegerent of Heaven above. These dimensions of Confucius's saying should not be overlooked. All Confucian morality, as we have seen, emerges from relations with other people. It is impossible to practise *shu* except in relation to other people, just as virtue, as Confucius has told us, always has neighbours. (This is why I defined *zhong* earlier as "being honest with oneself *in dealing with others*"; one never finds any sort of action characterized as *zhong* unless it involves another human being.)

Moreover, the stipulation that we must act in accordance with our social role means that the right way to behave depends on our relationship with the person we are presently engaged with. There are no universally valid moral injunctions because no one is in the same social position at every instant of his or her life:[37] "The Master said: 'In his associations with the world, there is nothing that the noble man [invariably] affirms or denies. He is a participant in what is right'" (*Analects* 4.10). This confirms our earlier conclusion that for Yan Yuan to look, listen, speak, and move in accordance with the rites, he must analyse each new situation afresh and infer from it the right mode of conduct for that particular moment. If he is in the role of father, he has one set of moral demands to consider; if he is in the role of son, the rites call for a very different pattern of behaviour. And it is up to him, through conscientious moral reasoning, to determine *all* such obligations.

The last major element of Confucius's political philosophy is that people's obligations to their kin are greater than their obligation to the state.

The Lord of She 葉公 said to Confucius: "In our village there is one Upright Gong.[38] His father stole a sheep, so the son testified against him."

Confucius said: "The upright people of my village are different from this. The fathers are willing to conceal their sons; the sons are willing to conceal their fathers. Uprightness lies therein." *(Analects* 13.18)

Confucius's response was taken by opponents to mean that he condoned theft, and his later follower Mencius went on to discuss certain specific examples so as to emphasize that handling a criminal father can entail significant hardship for the son (e.g. *Mencius* 7A.35). A son's obligation to his father includes not just protecting him from the arm of the law, but also expostulating with him when he believes his father's conduct is reprehensible. What Confucius means to say by this example is not that the son should welcome his father's thievery, but that he is misguided if he thinks he owes more to the faceless state than to the father who reared and raised him. Moral development begins in the family and only then radiates outwards to the rest of the world (as Mencius, again, would soon emphasize). Moral influence cannot be turned in the other direction.

Confucius recognizes that serving parents can be difficult: "The Master said: 'In serving your parents, remonstrate slightly. If you see that they do not intend to follow [your advice], remain respectful and do not disobey. Toil and do not complain'" *(Analects* 4.18). The remonstrance is indispensable; "acting as a son" must include raising controversial issues with one's parents whenever necessary. But imperfect parents are not always persuaded to mend their ways, and Confucius does not accept taking parents' mistakes as grounds for losing one's filial respect. "Toil and do not complain": you may know you are in the right, but if you have done everything you can to make your case, and your parents are intractable, you must endure your lot. No one ever said that life as a committed Confucian would be easy:

The Master said: "Young men are to be filial at home, courteous when abroad. They are to be careful and trustworthy; they are to overflow with love of the multitude and be intimate with humanity. If they have energy left over from their actions, then they use it to study refinements."

(*Analects* 1.6)

"Refinements" are pursuits such as literature and archery that are not directly related to moral practice, and these are permissible only if there is time and energy left over for them. One can survive, if necessary, without literature or archery, but no one can live without morality.

Two final themes before concluding this chapter. First, the opening line of the *Analects* merits comment:

> The Master said: "To study and then practise [what you have learned] at the right time – is this not a delight? To have friends come from distant places – is this not a joy? To be unknown by others, and yet not to be indignant – is this not a noble man?" (*Analects* 1.1)

It is only fitting that a philosopher who regards morality as a matter of thinking first but then *acting* appropriately should insist that study is incomplete without timely application. Moral practice cannot exist in isolation from other human beings, and thus self-cultivation that does not demonstrably affect the rest of the world is trivial. Evidently some of Confucius's disciples questioned their teacher on this account, arguing that, by teaching on the sidelines instead of throwing himself into the riotous political theatre, Confucius was betraying his own tenets. But he had a response:

> Zigong said: "There is a beautiful jade here. Should we enclose it in a case and store it, or should we seek a good price and sell it?"
> The Master said: "Sell it! Sell it! I am waiting for the right price." (*Analects* 9.12)

Inasmuch as Zigong went on to have a notable worldly career,[39] he is the right disciple to have asked this question. Confucius means to say that he would relish the opportunity to serve in government, but he will not do so until the regime has become worthy of his support. As long as his services are undervalued, he will keep himself off the labour market.

Moreover, carrying on with equanimity in an unappreciative, if not outright contemptuous, world is a major theme in Confucian philosophy; Confucius returns to it repeatedly,[40] and we shall see Mencius address it as well. The ability to rise above the carping of the unenlightened is born of the self-assurance that comes of rigorously assessing one's own conduct and satisfying oneself that one has truly lived up to the demands of one's conscience. But Confucius's self-confidence reached a level that may alienate modern readers, for there are suggestions that he thought Heaven itself supported his didactic mission:[41]

> The Master was terrorized in Kuang. He said: "Since the death of King Wen 文王, has Culture not still been here? If Heaven were about to let This Culture die, then I, a later mortal, would not be able to partake of This Culture. Since Heaven has not let This Culture die, what can the people of Kuang do to me?"　　　　　　　　　　(*Analects* 9.5)

Such statements problematize Confucius's claim that "at fifty, I knew Heaven's Mandate".[42] He seems to have been convinced that Heaven put him on this earth in order to teach mankind "This Culture" (*siwen* 斯文). And for most of Chinese history, posterity shared this belief.

TWO

Interlude: *Great Learning* and *Canon of Filial Piety*

Before turning to Mencius, it behoves us to examine two texts that cannot be dated precisely, but whose influence on the Confucian tradition has been enormous. Although Mencius may not have read these texts in their present form, he surely knew – and agreed with – the principles that they impart.

Great Learning (*Daxue* 大學) appears today as a chapter in a collection called *Ritual Records* (*Liji* 禮記), which contains texts of diverse date. The received version of the *Ritual Records* is probably relatively late (no earlier than the Han dynasty, and perhaps even later than that), but recent discoveries have confirmed that it includes some genuinely old material. *Jet-Black Robes* (*Ziyi* 緇衣), for example, had long been known from the *Ritual Records*, and was discovered in 1993 in a tomb dated to *c.*300 BCE at Guodian 郭店, and is also one of several manuscripts of unknown origin, but of similar date, recently purchased by the Shanghai Museum. The Guodian and Shanghai Museum recensions of *Jet-Black Robes* are slightly different from that of the *Ritual Records*, but are similar enough that there is no doubt we are dealing with one and the same text (a series of pronouncements attributed to an unnamed master).

There are too few clues, either internal or external, to permit any firm dating of *Great Learning*, but the text is indispensable for two reasons: first, its authority in later centuries was unquestioned, and second, it tidily encapsulates a quintessentially Confucian understanding of the connection between self-cultivation and moral governance. It is brief enough to be quoted here in full.

The Way of great learning lies in making brilliant one's brilliant virtue, in being intimate with the people, and in coming to rest in supreme goodness. After one knows one's resting place, one is settled; after one is settled, one can be tranquil; after one is tranquil, one can be at peace; after one is at peace, one can deliberate; after one deliberates, one can attain [the Way]. Things have their roots and branches; affairs have their beginnings and endings. If one knows what comes first and what comes last, one will be close to the Way.

Because the ancients desired to make their brilliant virtue shine throughout the world, they first ordered their states; desiring to order their states, they first regulated their families; desiring to regulate their families, they first cultivated themselves; desiring to cultivate themselves, they first rectified their hearts; desiring to rectify their hearts, they first made their intentions sincere; desiring to make their intentions sincere, they first brought about knowledge. Bringing about knowledge lies in investigating things. After things are investigated, knowledge is brought about; after knowledge is brought about, one's intentions are sincere; after one's intentions are sincere, one's heart is rectified; after one's heart is rectified, one cultivates oneself; after one has cultivated oneself, one's family is regulated; after one's family is regulated, the state is ordered; after the state is ordered, the world is at peace.

From the Son of Heaven down to the common people, [everyone] takes this as primary; all must take self-cultivation as their root. For the roots to be disordered and the branches ordered – this will not occur. There has never been a case [that ended well?] in which one neglected what should be emphasized and emphasized what should be neglected.[1]

The middle paragraph, the core of the text, narrates by *sorites* how to bring about peace in the world: one must go back logically, step by step, to the elemental act of "investigating things" – as the opaque phrase *gewu* 格物 is usually understood. It can also mean "to make things arrive" or "to come to things"; since the stage of *gewu* is obviously pivotal in this text, commentators have been debating its precise meaning for centuries. Confucians of a rationalist bent have held that it means understanding the underlying patterns of the cosmos by studying the rhythms and correspondences of things in nature. Then one attains knowledge, whereupon one can make one's intentions sincere, rectify one's heart, cultivate oneself, regulate one's family, order one's state and finally bring peace to the world.

Great Learning not only affirms that the ultimate end of the Confucian moral project, namely good government in all quarters of the world, can be achieved in this manner, but also implies that it cannot be achieved by any *other* process. The only way to achieve world peace is to begin by cultivating yourself, and then spread your morality outwards, through your own family, to your body politic around you and finally the rest of the world. Nothing will be accomplished by going in the other direction.

Mencius's familiarity with this idea is evident from two juxtaposed passages, 4A.4 and 4A.5:

> Mencius said: "If you love others, but they are not intimate [with you], reflect on your humanity; if you bring order to others, but they are not orderly, reflect on your wisdom; if you treat others with ritual, but they do not respond, reflect on your reverence. Whenever your actions are unsuccessful, you must reflect and seek [the cause] in yourself. If your person is rectified, the world will come home to you. It is said in the *Odes*: 'Forever may he live up to the Mandate [i.e. of Heaven], and seek for himself many blessings.'"[2]
>
> (*Mencius* 4A.4)

> Mencius said: "There is an enduring adage among the people; they say: 'The world, the state, the family.' The root of

> the world is in the state; the root of the state is in the family; and the root of the family is in the self." (*Mencius* 4A.5)

The conviction that self-cultivation and exemplary relations within the family form the basis of moral excellence in the wider world is fundamental to Confucian political thinking, and will be treated at greater length in Chapter 3. In imperial times, it was tirelessly invoked by literati who decried the government's attempts to control the populace by amoral administrative instruments.[3]

The privileged place of the family in the process of moral development is highlighted by the virtue of *xiao* 孝, "filial piety". The term goes back to the Bronze Age (and is not exclusive to Confucianism – indeed, virtually every Chinese ethical tradition had a concept of filial piety),[4] but before Confucius it had referred to reverence for all ancestors, and mostly had to do with due sacrifice on their behalf. As with so many other moral and religious terms, Confucius and his followers radically reinterpreted it[5] to mean appropriate behaviour *vis-à-vis* one's parents, and not only after their death. Merely providing sustenance was immediately disparaged as grotesquely inadequate:

> Ziyou 子游 [i.e. the disciple Yan Yan 言偃, b. 506 BCE] asked about filial piety. The Master said: "What is 'filial' nowadays refers to the ability to feed [one's parents]. Even dogs and horses can be fed. If one is not reverent, wherein lies the difference?" (*Analects* 2.7)

If one thinks filial piety consists primarily of feeding one's parents, and not in cultivating one's reverence, one is treating them like dogs and horses.

To Confucian minds, filial piety went together with the step-by-step approach to moral self-cultivation that we have seen in the *Great Learning*. If one of the first stages of moral development is attaining proper relations within the family, filial piety is indispensable to a person's progression from infancy to adulthood. Before you are prepared to face the world with its bewildering complexity, you learn your most basic moral lessons at home through filial piety.

Thus, despite much modern criticism of filial piety as an inherently backwards-looking notion,[6] the primary purpose of filial training was not to subordinate children to their parents, but to prepare them for an independent moral life of their own.[7]

This dimension is clear in the *Canon of Filial Piety* (*Xiaojing* 孝經), another work of uncertain date but probably in wide circulation by the third century BCE. The text is cast as a dialogue between Confucius and Master Zeng (who does little more than ask evocative questions). In the opening section, Confucius responds to Master Zeng by saying:

> "Filial piety is the root of virtue and the origin of instruction.[8] Sit back down and I shall lecture to you. You received your self, your body, your hair, and your skin from your mother and father: not daring to destroy or injure [these gifts] is the beginning of filial piety. Establishing oneself, practising the Way, and displaying one's name unto later generations in order to manifest one's mother and father is the end of filial piety. The beginning of filial piety is serving one's parents; the middle is serving one's ruler; the end is establishing oneself. It is said in the 'Greater Elegantiae' [of the *Odes*]: 'Why do you not remember your ancestors and cultivate your virtue?'"[9]   (*Canon of Filial Piety* 1)

Filial piety naturally involves gratitude and respect for the parents who brought one into the world, but it would be a grave mistake to forget the statement that the end of filial piety is establishing *oneself*. For it is one's own renown, and not mindless service, that brings the greatest glory on one's parents. Indeed, the *Canon of Filial Piety* emphasizes that, as Confucius intimated, true filial devotion compels children to remonstrate with their parents in cases of genuine moral disagreement:

> Master Zeng said: "Regarding kindness and love, reverence and respect, securing one's parents, and displaying one's name, I have heard your command. I venture to ask:

If a son follows his father's decrees, can that be called 'filial piety'?"

The Master said: "What kind of talk is this? What kind of talk is this? In the past, the Son of Heaven had seven ministers to expostulate with him so that he would not lose the world even if he [were about to act] without the Way. The feudal lords had five ministers to expostulate with them so that they would not lose their states even if they [were about to act] without the Way. The grand masters had three ministers to expostulate with them so that they would not lose their families even if they [intended to act] without the Way. If a man-of-service has friends to expostulate with him, he will not depart from his illustrious virtue; if a father has a son to expostulate with him, he will not fall into unrighteousness. Thus whenever there is unrighteousness, a son cannot but expostulate with his father and a minister cannot but expostulate with his lord. Thus whenever there is unrighteousness, one expostulates about it. To follow one's father's decrees – how can that be filial piety?"

(Canon of Filial Piety 15)

Surely there is no better evidence that the practice of filial piety was not intended "to turn China into a big factory for the manufacturing of obedient subjects" 把中國弄成一個「製造順民的大工廠」, as the critic Wu Yu 吳虞 (1871–1949) alleged.[10] Rather, the Confucian understanding is that filial discipline at home launches children on the long journey of moral self-cultivation. The later sections of the *Canon of Filial Piety* affirm repeatedly that filial piety is to be regarded as the cornerstone of moral training and virtuous government.

Master Zeng said: "Very great is filial piety!"

The Master said: "Filial piety is the warp[11] of Heaven, the appropriate [standard] of Earth, and the practice of the people. The people take the warp of Heaven as their pattern; the brilliance of patterning oneself after Heaven and the benefits of complying with Earth are used to instruct the world. Thus [a ruler's] act of instruction is completed without being strict and his government is ordered without being stern. The Former Kings saw the ability of instruction to transform the people, so they led them with broad love, and there were none among the people who abandoned their parents. [The Kings] explained virtue and righteousness to them, and the people were aroused to practise it. [The Kings] led them using reverence and deference, and the people did not contend [with each other]. [The Kings] led them using ritual and music, and the people were harmonious and friendly. [The Kings] showed them what to like and dislike, and the people knew what was forbidden. It is said in the *Odes*: 'Awesome Master Yin! The people all look to you.'"[12]

(*Canon of Filial Piety* 7)

And similarly:

What more is there in the virtue of a Sage than filial piety? Thus intimacy [towards one's parents] is born when one is beneath [one's parents'] knees; in nurturing one's father and mother, one becomes more solemn everyday. The Sages accord with this solemnity in order to teach reverence; they accord with intimacy in order to teach love. … They accord with the root. The Way of father and son is imparted from Heaven, [as is] the righteous [relationship] between lord and subject. One's father and mother give birth to one: there is no greater form of continuity than this. One's lord and parents draw near to one: there is no richer form of kindness than this. Thus those who do not love their parents but love other people are called "perverters of virtue". Those who do not revere their parents but revere other people are called "perverters of ritual".   (*Canon of Filial Piety* 9)

With the claim that those who dare to elevate outsiders above their own parents are perverters of virtue and ritual, we are finally prepared to tackle Mencius, for such were (in Mencius's view) the unacceptable teachings of a philosopher who came between Confucius and Mencius, namely Mo Di. Mo and his followers argued, essentially, that what is right is what is most profitable for human beings as a community. Since "partiality" (*bie* 別) engenders the desire to enrich oneself (and one's family and friends) at the expense of others, it is to be condemned; the only laudable mode of behaviour is impartiality (*jian* 兼), or treating everyone in the world alike. Mo Di believed that impartiality was, if paradoxically, the highest form of filial piety, because it guaranteed that others would treat one's own father with dignity and respect. But Mencius could not abide this justification; to him, Mohist "impartiality" was tantamount to rejecting all familial bonds and treating one's own father as a stranger. And nothing could be further from the Confucian idea that moral cultivation begins in the home at one's parents' knees.

THREE

Mencius

Mencius is said by the historian Sima Qian 司馬遷 (145?–86? BCE) to have studied with Confucius's grandson, Zisi 子思 (483?–402? BCE), but the latter's dates make this unlikely. What is more probable is that Mencius, more than any other Chinese philosopher of the fourth century BCE, was thought to further the Confucian mission and thereby inherit the mantle of Confucius himself. In later centuries, Neo-Confucians regarded him as the last sage.

Modern students of Mencius are faced with many of the same problems as with Confucius. Mencius did not write the surviving repository of his teachings, the eponymous *Mencius*, which was compiled after his death and edited in its present form by the commentator Zhao Qi 趙岐 (d. 201 CE). Zhao took a text in eleven sections and eliminated four that he considered inferior, leaving the *Mencius* in seven books that we know today. One can only guess how different our conception of Mencius would be if we could read the parts that Zhao excised. (Throughout imperial history, opportunists tried to present some "newly discovered" text as the four lost books of *Mencius*, but these were always shown to be forgeries.)

And once again there are few external sources that one can use to corroborate details of Mencius's life.[1] Like Confucius, Mencius was known mostly as a teacher who had audiences with some powerful rulers, but did not assume significant office himself. At times, he was criticized for inaction:

> Chunyu Kun 淳于髡 [fl. 320–311 BCE] said: "Is it ritually correct that when males and females give and take, they are not to touch each other?"
>
> Mencius said: "That is ritually correct."
>
> [Chunyu Kun] said: "If one's sister-in-law is drowning, does one extend one's hand to her?"
>
> [Mencius] said: "One who does not extend [his hand] when his sister-in-law is drowning is a jackal or a wolf. It is ritually correct that when males and females give and take, they are not to touch each other, but to extend one's hand to one's sister-in-law when she is drowning – that is *quan* 權 [i.e. disregarding an otherwise binding norm in exigent circumstances]."[2]
>
> [Chunyu Kun] said: "Now the world is drowning; sir, why do you not extend [yourself]?"
>
> [Mencius] said: "If the world is drowning, I extend the Way to it; if my sister-in-law is drowning, I extend my hand to her. Sir, do you want me to extend my hand to the world?"
>
> (Mencius 4A.17)

Chunyu Kun, an able speaker whom later generations often misunderstood, was hardly so barbaric as to suggest that one stand idly by while one's sister-in-law is washed away merely because the ritual codes proscribe physical contact between a man and his brother's wife. Rather, his purpose was to convey that the world is drowning, and that Mencius, who had a reputation as an admirer of ritual, might do well to abandon his devotion to such niceties and take some bold action.

Some revealing information about Mencius as a man comes from his own words; to be sure, this is biased material, but it sheds light on how he conceived of his mission. First, there is his famous comment about his "flood-like *qi*" (*haoran zhi qi* 浩然之氣):

[The disciple Gongsun Chou 公孫丑] asked: "I venture to ask: wherein lie your strengths, Master?"

[Mencius] said: "I know words. I am good at nourishing my flood-like *qi*."

"I venture to ask: What do you mean by 'flood-like *qi*'?"

"It is difficult to say. It is the kind of *qi* that is greatest and firmest. If it is nourished with uprightness and is not damaged, it fills in the space between Heaven and Earth. It is the kind of *qi* that is the consort of righteousness and the Way. Without it, [the body] starves. It is engendered by the accumulation of righteousness and is not obtained through sporadic righteousness. If there is something in one's actions that does not satisfy the heart, then [the flood-like *qi*] starves. Thus I say: Master Gao 告子 never knew righteousness, because he considered it external. You must take it as your duty and not let it out of your heart.[3] Do not let it out of your heart and do not 'help it grow'. Do not be like the man of Song. There was a man of Song who was sorry that his sprouts were not growing and pulled them up. He came home appearing weary and said to his people: 'Today I am worn out; I have helped my sprouts grow.' His son rushed out and went to look; the sprouts were all withered. There are few people in the world who do not 'help their sprouts grow'. Those who abandon them, thinking that they cannot [do anything to] benefit them, do not weed their sprouts. Those who 'help them grow' pull up their sprouts; not only are they not [doing anything to] benefit them – they are also damaging them."   (*Mencius* 2A.2)

Master Gao was an older contemporary of Mencius, probably a Confucian of a rival faction, with whom Mencius had an important debate that will be analysed further below.

This opaque passage has been the subject of much intellectual dispute, and there can be no definitive interpretation, inasmuch as Mencius himself concedes that "flood-like *qi*" is difficult to explain. *Qi* is a term that Confucius had very rarely used; literally it means "breath" or "vapour", but is used by most ancient philosophers as a generic term for matter. All material in the world is made up of *qi*. Naturally *qi* comes in different qualities: tables or chairs are not capable of the same feats as sentient beings. The highest form of *qi* was thought to reside in human beings, but there too grades must vary, for some people seem to be inherently more talented than others.

In his discussion of *qi*, Mencius departs from his contemporaries' understanding of the concept[4] by stating that the method of cultivating *qi* lies in regular moral practice: "it is engendered by the accumulation of righteousness and is not obtained through sporadic righteousness". Before this, tending one's *qi* was usually understood as a physical process. For Mencius, if one accumulates righteousness day in and day out, the result will be the improvement of one's *qi*. Mencius is saying that morality is good for your health. Confucius never made a claim remotely resembling this.

Moreover, Mencius's distinction between *engendering* flood-like *qi* by accumulating righteousness and trying *to obtain* it through sporadic acts highlights another characteristic theme in his philosophy: morality has to be made to grow naturally and cannot be seized like a foreign object. The closing analogy of the foolish husbandman who tried "to help his sprouts grow" drives the point home. We foster our morality by providing it with nourishing conditions, and then watching it take root. We only harm ourselves if we treat morality as something external to the self.

Mencius's second informative comment about himself comes in response to his disciple's observation that others call him "fond of disputation" (*haobian* 好辯). Mencius's response was: "How could I be fond of disputation? I simply cannot avoid it". He saw himself as the defender of the Confucian tradition in the face of new heterodoxies threatening to overwhelm it:

> The words of Yang Zhu 楊朱 and Mo Di swell across the world. [People's] words throughout the world find their home in Mo if they do not do so in Yang. Mr Yang's [credo] is 'For Me!' – there is no ruler in that. Mr Mo's [credo] is 'Universal Love!' – there is no father in that. To be with-

out ruler or father is to be a beast. ... If the ways of Yang and Mo are not quelled and the Way of Confucius not made manifest, then these heterodox propositions will delude the people, and will fully obstruct humanity and righteousness. When humanity and righteousness are completely obstructed, then they will lead beasts to eat people, and people will eat each other.

I am alarmed by this, and defend the Way of the Former Kings. I resist Yang and Mo and banish their licentious statements, so that their heterodox propositions have no opportunity to intrude. If they intrude on [people's] hearts, then they will damage their affairs; if they intrude on their affairs, then they will damage the government. When a sage rises again, he will not alter my words. (*Mencius* 3B.9)

Yang Zhu was a peripheral figure whose philosophy later scholars tried (mostly unsuccessfully) to reconstruct, on the assumption that if Mencius mentioned him as one of the two great heretics in the world, he must have been an important philosopher. Suffice it to say that there are only three or four references to Yang Zhu in the entire surviving pre-imperial literature, all of them in partisan sources. What Mencius meant by "For Me!" as Yang's credo is not entirely clear, but it is usually taken to mean that Yang thought no action is worthwhile unless it benefits the self, and therefore would not help the rest of the world if it caused him any hardship.[5]

Mo Di's philosophy, on the other hand, is well understood, because there are ample external sources confirming the tenets of the Mohist school, and the surviving anthology of their teachings, the *Mozi*, is long and detailed. We have seen earlier why Mencius anathematized it: the notion that morality lies in denying special relationships among family members reviled him as contrary to nature itself. Mencius's full refutation of Mohist ethics is justly celebrated:

The Mohist Yi Zhi 夷之 sought an audience with Mencius through [his disciple] Xu Bi. Mencius said: "I am certainly willing to have an audience with him, but now I am slightly ill. When my illness recedes, I shall go to see him; Master Yi need not come here." On another day, he sought an audience with Mencius again. Mencius said: "Today I can see him. If I do not correct him, the Way will not be apparent. So let me correct him. I have heard that Master Yi is a Mohist. According to the Mohist precepts on funerals, sparseness is their way. If Master Yi thinks that he can change the world with [the Mohist precepts], then would he not consider them correct and would he not honour them? But Master Yi buried his own parents richly, and thus served his parents in a way that he considers base."

Master Xu told Master Yi about this, and Master Yi said: "According to the Way of the Confucians, the ancients 'were as though protecting a baby'. What does this refer to? To me, it means to love without differences of degree, but the practice [i.e. of love] begins with one's parents."

Master Xu told Mencius about this, and Mencius said: "Does Master Yi really think that a person's closeness to his elder brother's child is equal to his closeness to his neighbour's baby? What we can take from his [teachings] is this. If a baby were crawling around and were about to fall into a well, this would not be the fault of the baby. Moreover, when Heaven engenders creatures, it gives them one base, but Master Yi has two bases. This is the cause [of his errors].

"In earliest times, there were those who did not bury their parents. When their parents died, they carried them and cast them into a ditch. On another day, they passed by [and saw] that foxes and wildcats had eaten [their parents' corpses] and that flies and gnats were gnawing at them. Their foreheads became sweaty, and they glanced away so as not to see. Now as for their sweat – it was not that they were sweating for other people. The [emotions] of their innermost heart reached their faces and eyes; they went home forthwith, and [came back] to cover [the corpses] with overturned baskets and shovels. If covering them was indeed right, then the filial son and humane person must also be with the Way in covering their parents."

Master Xu told Master Yi about this, and Master Yi was pensive for a while. Then he said: "He has taught me."

(Mencius 3A.5)

What is meant by the "two bases" is not directly explained, but probably refers to the fact that Yi Zhi espoused one set of views regarding appropriate burial customs, but then went ahead and buried his parents as his conscience guided him, even though this violated Mohist doctrine. In Mencius's view, Yi Zhi was well served by following his unstated impulses, since they were pushing him in the right direction: we love our parents and wish to bury them decorously because that is how human beings ought to feel. But it follows that we must abandon Mohism because it prescribes behaviour incompatible with humane instincts.[6]

The notion that the bedrock of morality lies within natural human impulses is typical of Mencius, and informs his most important area of departure from Confucius: his theory of human nature. Mencius is famous for having argued that human nature is good, but his position is more complex than it may seem, and requires careful unravelling. Mencius believed that all human beings are endowed by Heaven with what he called the "Four Beginnings" (*siduan* 四端) of virtue. These are lodged in the heart (which was, we must remember, also taken to be the locus of mental processes, as we regard the brain today).[7] Mencius's proof is that on occasions where we are presented with a sudden and unforeseen moral crisis, and we have no opportunity for calculating how we should act (or how outsiders will judge us for acting), we unthinkingly act with compassion. His best-known illustration is the analogy of an infant about to fall into a well:

Mencius said: "All people have a heart that cannot bear [the suffering] of others. The Former Kings had a heart that could not bear [the suffering] of others, and thus had a government that could not bear [the suffering] of others. By using a heart that cannot bear [the suffering] of others to put into practice a government that cannot bear [the suffering] of others, ruling the world is [as easy as] moving it around in one's palm.

"What is meant by 'All people have a heart that cannot bear [the suffering] of others' is as follows. Suppose a person suddenly saw a child about to fall into a well. Everyone [in such a situation] would have a frightened, compassionate heart, not in order to ingratiate himself with the child's parents, not because he wants praise from his neighbours and friends, and not because he would hate to have the reputation [of one who would not save an innocent child]. From this we see: Whoever lacks a commiserating heart is not human. Whoever lacks a heart of shame is not human. Whoever lacks a heart of deference is not human. Whoever lacks a heart of right and wrong is not human. The heart of commiseration is the beginning of humanity. The heart of shame is the beginning of righteousness. The heart of deference is the beginning of ritual. The heart of right and wrong is the beginning of wisdom."

(*Mencius* 2A.6)

Even people with serious moral failings can be capable of such impulsive demonstrations of compassion. King Xuan of Qi 齊宣王 (r. 319–310 BCE), for example, was an imperfect monarch whom Mencius criticized on many counts, but at one juncture Mencius pointed out that even he displayed his basic moral orientation at an unexpected moment:

Mencius said: "I have heard that Hu He said: 'The King was sitting at the top of the hall. There was someone with a sacrificial ox passing by the bottom of the hall. The King saw him, and said: What ox is that? The man answered: We are going to use it for a blood-sacrifice with a bell. The King said: Leave it; I cannot bear its fearful expression. It is like that of an innocent person approaching the execution-ground. The man answered: Then will you do away with the blood-sacrifice and bell? The King said: How can I do away with that? Change it for a sheep.' I am not aware whether that happened."

The King said: "It happened."

Mencius said: "This type of heart is sufficient for a [true] king. The Hundred Clans all thought that you begrudged [the expense of the animal], but I know surely that it was because you could not bear the sight."

The King said: "That is so. But there was indeed [an appearance] of what the Hundred Clans supposed. Although the state of Qi is narrow and small, how would I begrudge one ox? Since I could not bear its frightened appearance – like that of an innocent person approaching the execution-ground – I exchanged it for a sheep."

"Your Majesty, do not think it strange that the Hundred Clans thought you begrudged [the expense]. When you exchanged a large [animal] for a small one, how would they know [the real reason]? If you felt compassion on account of its [appearance as] an innocent person approaching the execution-ground, then what was there to choose between an ox and a sheep?"

The King laughed and said: "Indeed! What was in my heart? I did not begrudge the expense, but I exchanged it for a sheep. It was appropriate that the Hundred Clans called me stingy!"

"Do not be hurt by it. [Your conduct] was an instantiation of humanity. You saw the ox; you did not see the sheep. With regard to beasts, the noble man [acts] as follows. When he sees them alive, he cannot bear to see them die. When he hears their sounds, he cannot bear to eat their flesh. Therefore the noble man keeps a distance from the kitchen."

(*Mencius* 1A.7)

Although most observers thought the King merely wanted to economize by sacrificing a sheep instead of an ox, Mencius discerns that he insisted on saving the ox because he could not bear to see his "fearful expression", whereas the sheep, out of sight in its pen, had no direct effect on his emotions. Presumably, if the King had seen the sheep as well, he would have been unable to consign it to the blood-sacrifice either.

The King becomes mightily self-satisfied when he hears Mencius's analysis of his conduct, asking how the philosopher could have known that his heart corresponds to that of a true king. Mencius immediately rebukes him:

> [Mencius] said: "If there were someone who responded to you, saying: 'My strength is sufficient to lift a hundred *jun* [a unit of weight], but not sufficient to lift a single feather; my keenness of sight is sufficient to detect the tip of an autumn hair [i.e. an animal's new winter coat], but I cannot see a cartload of firewood', would Your Majesty accept this?"
>
> [The King] said: "No."
>
> "Now your grace is sufficient to reach birds and beasts, but your merit does not extend to the Hundred Surnames – why indeed is this? In such a case, not lifting a single feather is a matter of not using one's strength; not seeing a cartload of firewood is a matter of not using one's keenness of sight. Not protecting the Hundred Surnames is a matter of not using your grace. Thus your Majesty is not a true king because you do not act as one; it is not because you are unable."
>
> (*Mencius* 1A.7)

In other words, the basic impulse that Mencius has just praised as the foundation of morality is not morality itself. King Xuan has demonstrated not that he is a true king, but that he is capable of becoming one. As he is manifestly not a true king, he has failed only because he has not done what is necessary to become one. If he is capable of treating sacrificial oxen with compassion, how much more appropriate would it be for him to treat his subjects with the same grace?

After enumerating the Four Beginnings of humanity, righteousness, ritual and wisdom, Mencius intones the same warning:

"Humans have these Four Beginnings as we have our four limbs. To have these Four Beginnings and say that one is incapable [i.e. of developing them] is to make oneself into a brigand; to say that one's lord is incapable [of developing them] is to make one's lord into a brigand. Since we all have these Four Beginnings within ourselves, if we know to broaden them all and make them full, then it is like a fire beginning to blaze, or a spring beginning to rise up. If one can make them full, they will be sufficient to protect the Four Seas; if one cannot make them full, they will not be sufficient [even] to serve one's father and mother."   (*Mencius* 2A.6)

In line with his understanding of moral self-cultivation as constitutive of physical self-cultivation, Mencius asserts that the Four Beginnings are as fundamental to the human constitution as the four limbs. No one can claim that he or she lacks the Four Beginnings, for Heaven has endowed all of us with them. The most we can say is that we have declined to develop them, and thus have allowed ourselves to devolve into evil. We cannot pretend that we were born as "brigands".[8]

Moral self-cultivation, then, is a matter of "extending" (*da* 達 or *tui* 推) the incipient virtue lying in each person's heart:[9]

Mencius said: "What people can do without having learned it is their innate ability; what they know without thinking is their innate knowledge. There are no young children who do not know to love their parents; when they have grown, there are none who do not know to respect their elder brothers. To be intimate with one's parents is humanity; to respect one's elders is righteousness. There is no other [task] but to extend this to the rest of the world."   (*Mencius* 7A.15)[10]

Thus, as A. C. Graham compellingly argued,[11] when Mencius claims that human *xing* 性 is good, he means not that we are born good, and certainly not that our nature as adults is necessarily good, but that we all have the capacity to become good – or, more strongly stated, that goodness is the state we are expected to attain if we are provided with the proper nurturing environment. For this is how Mencius consistently employs the keyword *xing*: as the ideal state than an organism is expected to attain under the right conditions.

This nuance is crucial, because it underlies the entire discussion of *xing* in Book 6A.[12] It begins with an exchange with Master Gao, who had a radically different understanding of the term: *xing* refers to all inborn faculties and impulses in an organism. "[Appetite for] food and sex is the *xing*", he said (*Mencius* 6A.4). Mencius objected:

> Gaozi said: "What is inborn is called *xing*."
> Mencius said: "Is what is inborn called *xing* in the way that white is called 'white'?"
> [Gaozi] said: "It is so."
> "Is the whiteness of white feathers like the whiteness of white snow; is the whiteness of white snow like the whiteness of white jade?"
> [Gaozi] said: "It is so."
> "Then is the *xing* of a dog like the *xing* of an ox; is the *xing* of an ox like the *xing* of a human being?"   (*Mencius* 6A.3)

It was never clear to traditional commentators precisely what Mencius accomplished in this exchange.[13] If anything, by resorting to such questionable hypostatizations as "the whiteness of white feathers", his argument may be thought to bear out the charge that he was "fond of disputation". But the recent discovery of Confucian manuscripts from an ancient tomb, dated to *c.*300 BCE, reveals what was at stake. Named after Guodian, the modern town where the tomb was found, this corpus includes a text called *The* Xing *Emerges from the Endowment*, which defines *xing* as the set of inborn characteristics shared by all members of a species. The similarity of the Guodian manuscripts to the philosophical views that can be tentatively ascribed to Master Gao has led some scholars to postulate a sectarian connection between the two. While this cannot be confirmed with the available evidence, it is clear that Master Gao adopted what must have been a commonplace definition – one that

Mencius simply could not accept because of his own peculiar usage of *xing* as the ideal state that an organism should attain in a conducive environment. As far as Mencius was concerned, by asserting that "what is inborn is called *xing*", Master Gao effectively denied that there is a fundamental difference between human beings and animals. Animals, after all, desire food and sex as much as humans do. The debate is best understood as a scholastic dispute: Master Gao belongs to a group that understood *xing* in a manner intolerable to Mencius. (And the Guodian manuscripts suggest, contrary to all subsequent orthodoxy, that it may have been Mencius's usage of *xing*, not that of Master Gao, that was considered eccentric in ancient times.)

Confucius himself had rarely discussed *xing*; indeed, according to Zigong, *xing* is one of the concepts that one could never hear Confucius speak of (*Analects* 5.12). In *Analects* 17.2 – one of the suspiciously late sections – Confucius declares: "By their *xing*, people are close to each other. They grow distant from each other through practice." This seems craftily worded so as not to be easily mapped onto the later spectrum of opinions about *xing*: it could mean, in line with Master Gao, that people are born with essentially the same faculties and desires, but then diverge because of habits and other forms of acculturation; or it could mean, in line with Mencius, that people are born with the same fundamental tendency towards goodness, but that not everybody does the necessary legwork to develop these roots into the flourishing state of goodness that Mencius wanted us to attain.

Thus modern readers are sometimes puzzled as to why Mencius devoted so much energy to arguing over the definitions of novel technical terms. Why not simply use uncontested terminology and avoid all the controversy? Two observations are in order. First, in Mencius's debate with Master Gao we see something that could not have existed in Confucius's time: rival Confucian camps with mutually incompatible doctrinal stances. In the days of Confucius and his disciples, there was one living and unquestioned authority, whose philosophy each follower struggled to understand. Now, some two centuries later, the sole unquestioned authority was long dead, and opponents like Mencius and Master Gao could regard themselves as authentically Confucian and each other as regrettably misguided.

Second, by redefining *xing* in his peculiar fashion, Mencius was able to cast human beings not as static things with certain characteristics determined by birth, but as growing organisms constantly tending toward higher planes of moral awareness. He regarded humanity not as a matter of being, but as a matter of becoming, to use a Greek sort of distinction.[14] Mencius may have wanted to convey obliquely that, where moral development is concerned, human beings can never stand still.

The rest of Book 6A is devoted to tying up the loose ends of the theory of *xing*. If we are all born with the Four Beginnings of virtue in the same way that we are born with four limbs, one might ask why some people become good and others do not.

> Mencius said: "The trees of Ox Mountain were once beautiful. Because it was in the suburbs of a great city, with axes and hatchets chopping at it, could it remain beautiful? With the respite that [the mountain] was afforded by the nights,[15] and the moisture of the rain and dew, it was not without buds and sprouts that grew on it; but then the cattle and goats came to pasture there. That is why it is so bald. People see its baldness, and suppose that it never had timber on it. Is this the *xing* of the mountain?

> "Even what exists within human beings – are we without a heart of humanity and righteousness? The manner in which we let go of our good hearts is like axes and hatchets with respect to trees. If [the trees] are chopped down every morning, can they remain beautiful? With the respite that we are afforded by the nights,[16] and the [restorative influence] of the morning air, our likes and dislikes are close to those of other people. [But the power of this restorative process] is slight, and it is fettered and destroyed by what takes place during the day. When this fettering is repeated again and again, the [restorative] nocturnal airs are insufficient to preserve [our goodness]. If the nocturnal air is

insufficient to preserve [our goodness], then we are not far from being unruly beasts. People see our bestiality, and suppose that there was never any ability[17] in us. Is this human *xing*?

"Thus, if it obtains its nourishment, no creature will fail to grow; if it loses its nourishment, no creature will fail to decay." (*Mencius* 6A.8)

Note that, once again, the imagery is taken from the botanical world. Mountains may be lush or bald, just as people may be good or bad, but it is a mistake to assume that the mountain's *xing* is anything other than to be lush, for this is the state it would attain with the right "nourishment". Thus it is no refutation of Mencius's theory to point out that Ox Mountain is currently bald – or that some people are bad; Mencius's response is that Ox Mountain, like a bad person, has been denied its due "nourishment".[18]

But this is not wholly satisfactory as an answer to the question of why some people become bad, because it does not explain how some people are fortunate enough to enjoy a nutritive environment, while others are not. Moreover, unless people bear some responsibility for settling themselves in the right environment, one might wrongly infer from the parable of Ox Mountain that becoming good or bad is just a matter of luck. "I am not to be blamed", a criminal might proclaim; "I am simply a product of my deleterious circumstances". Mencius does not fail to undercut this argument in a discussion with a disciple named Master Gongdu 公都子:

Master Gongdu asked: "We are all equally human. Why is it that some of us become great people, and some become lesser people?"

Mencius said: "Those who follow their greater parts become great people; those who follow their lesser parts become lesser people."

[Master Gongdu] said: "We are all equally human. Why is it that some people follow their greater parts, and some follow their lesser parts?"

[Mencius] said: "The organs of the ears and eyes do not think, and are blinded by objects. When an object interacts with another object, it simply leads it astray. But the organ of the heart thinks. If it thinks, it obtains its [object, i.e. morality]; if it does not think, it does not obtain it. These are what Heaven has imparted to us; if we first establish ourselves in the greater [parts], then the lesser ones cannot snatch [our attention]. To be a great person is nothing more than this."

(*Mencius* 6A.15)

The "greater part" is the heart, the "lesser parts" the sense organs (and perhaps other organs as well, such as the genitals). People who become good emphasize the greater part; people who become bad emphasize the lesser parts. But why do some people emphasize the greater part and others the lesser parts? Because those who emphasize the lesser parts are seduced by their own desires. Those who emphasize the greater part use the special function of the heart "to think" – Mencius always understands "thinking" (*si* 思) in a moral sense – and sincerely assess their own conduct. Most people cannot bear this degree of self-scrutiny, and simply avoid asking themselves whether their behaviour is truly reconcilable with morality; they must know, in their marrow, that the answer is no, but acknowledging this would force them to transcend the urges of their "lesser parts", which have led them thoroughly astray. Thus becoming good is not simply a matter of being born and raised in an environment that fosters our Four Beginnings; for if we find that our Four Beginnings have been devastated, we must, if we are to be honest, admit that we ourselves have had a hand in the devastation. In this respect, we are responsible for our own morality.

Mencius's conception of *xing* is essential to understanding his otherwise enigmatic pronouncements about "destiny" (*ming* 命):

Mencius said: "Those who exhaust their minds know their *xing*. If they know their *xing*, then they know Heaven. Preserving one's mind and nourishing one's *xing* is how one serves Heaven. Not being of two minds in the face of premature death or long life and cultivating oneself in order to await [one's fate] is how one establishes one's destiny."

Mencius said: "There is nothing that is not destined. One should compliantly receive one's proper [destiny]. Therefore those who know destiny do not stand by a precipitous wall. To die having exhausted the Way is proper destiny. To die in manacles and fetters is not proper destiny."

(*Mencius* 7A.1–2)

Mo Di had earlier criticized Confucius and his followers for being fatalists; by declaring that everything was "destined" (*ming*), Mohists argued, Confucians abandoned all hope of a theory of personal responsibility. What Confucians before Mencius thought about *ming* is difficult to reconstruct (according to the *Analects*, at least, Confucius had little to say about *ming* other than that, as we have seen, his mission was undeniably sanctioned by Heaven).

In Mencius's formulation, however, it is clear that the Mohist charge fails. For Mencius hardly agrees that a theory of *ming* has to be one of fatalism. Indeed, the very translation "destiny" can be misleading if we adopt the connotations of that word familiar from romantic literature and film (e.g. "The moment Algernon first mentioned to me that he had a friend called Ernest, I knew I was destined to love you").[19] To Mencius, destiny is not the fate that has been predetermined for us, but the exalted state that we are expected to attain through our own diligent labour. Our proper destiny is waiting for us, and if we fail to achieve it, we have only ourselves to blame.[20] We may have no control over our longevity or social status, but there is one thing we can do regardless of our lot in life: we can preserve our hearts, nourish our *xing*, and become moral paragons.

* * *

The best-known example of Mencius's belief in the rightness of basic human impulses is the parable of the baby about to fall into a well, but there are several others. In a difficult passage that is rarely discussed (*Mencius* 3B.10), Mencius and his friend Kuang Zhang 匡章 (i.e. the renowned general Tian Zhang 田章, fl. 334–295 BCE) consider the case of one Chen Zhongzi 陳仲子, a man so fastidious that he refused to live with his brother because he thought his brother's wealth was ill gotten, and once even forced himself to vomit a meal that his mother had cooked for him because he considered the meat unclean. Mencius's judgement was that if Chen's principles were pushed to their logical extremes, only an earthworm could live up to them. Human beings, unlike earthworms, have certain natural relationships with one another, and violating them on account of the ideals that one has constructed for oneself cannot possibly be right. However high-minded you may be, if your scruples prevent you from living with your brother, and lead you to vomit your mother's food, you have been waylaid by your specious sensibilities.

Other examples bear on Mencius's political philosophy. A sustained discussion with the aforementioned King Xuan of Qi is centred on the idea that human desires are inescapable. The stage is set by a report by an otherwise unknown Zhuang Bao 莊暴, who tells Mencius that he was unable to respond when the King told him of his fondness for music. What the King meant, presumably, is that talking about morality may be fine for philosophers, but lovers of the good life revel in music and cannot be persuaded to reform themselves. Mencius tells Zhuang Bao that he should have built on this basic human trait of the King's by urging him to share his pleasure with his people. Then they would rejoice whenever they heard the distant strains of his music (*Mencius* 1B.1).[21] Eventually Mencius had his own audience with the King, and asked why the King had not put good government into practice, if he applauded it in the abstract.

> The King said: "I have a weakness; I am fond of wealth."
> [Mencius] responded: "In the past, Gong Liu was fond of wealth. It is said in the *Odes*: 'He stocked and stored; he wrapped dry provisions in sacks and bags. Ah, he gathered in order to make [his people] eminent. With bows and arrows nocked, and shields, halberds, and axes brandished – then he commenced his advance.'[22] Those who stayed at home had stocked storehouses; those who advanced [with

him] had sacks of wrapped [provisions] – only then could he 'commence his march'. Your Majesty, if you love wealth, but share it with the Hundred Surnames, what [damage] will this cause you?"

The King said: "I have a weakness: I am fond of sex."

[Mencius] responded: "In the past, King Tai was fond of sex and loved his consort. It is said in the *Odes*: 'Ancient Lord Danfu came in the morning, galloping his horse; he followed the banks of the western rivers until he came to the foot of [Mount] Qi. Thither he brought Lady Jiang; he came and tarried there, making it his abode.'[23] At that time, there were no frustrated girls within [the home], no bachelors abroad. Your Majesty, if you love sex, but share it with the Hundred Surnames, what [damage] will this cause you?"

(*Mencius* 1B.5)

The King cannot use his love of wealth and sex as an excuse not to partake of Mencius's programme of moral cultivation; on the contrary, these urges only demonstrate his humanity, and should prompt him to extend his virtue throughout the domain by enabling his people to enjoy the same pleasures. Then he would be a king cherished by grateful subjects! Confucians never argued that desires are objectionable *per se* because one can hardly be human without desires; what is, however, subject to praise or blame is the manner in which one pursues those desires. King Xuan of Qi monopolizes his enjoyment of music, wealth and sex, whereas a more enlightened ruler would provide the people with the means to enjoy them alongside him.[24] As we shall see in Chapter 4, Xunzi would go on to build a metaphysically more complicated theory of desire, but he would have fully agreed with Mencius that human desires cannot (and should not) be extinguished. Instead, the Sages furnished humanity with suitable social and aesthetic forms through which they could gratify their physical and emotional desires.

Mencius never tolerates false pretexts or mere velleities when it comes to the serious business of moral self-cultivation.[25] If morality is your stated aim, you must pursue it with every ounce of energy;

otherwise, you may as well acknowledge that you do not care enough to do more. When King Hui of Liang 梁惠王 (i.e. King Hui of Wei 魏, r. 370–319 BCE) complains that he has "exhausted his heart" on behalf of his state, but his power has only decreased, Mencius compares him to a cowardly soldier who flees fifty paces on the battlefield, and looks down upon others who fled a full hundred paces (*Mencius* 1A.3). When Dai Yingzhi 戴盈之 (otherwise unknown) protests that it is fiscally inconvenient to reduce taxes before the following year, Mencius replies that this is like asking if it is all right not to stop stealing chickens until next year (*Mencius* 3B.8). And when King Xuan of Qi wishes to reduce ritually mandated mourning periods, and Gongsun Chou is inclined to allow this dereliction on the argument that observing an abbreviated mourning period is better than not observing any mourning period at all, Mencius's response is that this is like saying "Do it gently!" to someone who is twisting his elder brother's arm (*Mencius* 7A.39). Permitting such rationalizations only encourages people to destroy their own hearts, and a loyal minister must be his lord's unflinching moral guide (e.g. *Mencius* 1B.9).

* * *

Mencius's conception of government is similar to that of Confucius; the most important plank of his platform is that the purpose of government is the cultivation of morality – no more and no less. The best-known passage is the opening of the book:

> Mencius had an audience with King Hui of Liang. The King said: "Venerable man, you have not considered it [too] far to come here from a thousand *li*[26] away; surely you will have some means to profit my state?"
>
> Mencius responded: "Your Majesty, why must you speak of 'profit'? Indeed, I possess nothing more than humanity and righteousness. If the King says: 'How can I profit my state?' then the Grand Masters will say: 'How can I profit my family?' and the men-of-service and commoners will say: 'How can I profit myself?' Superiors and inferiors will wage

war on each other for profit and the state will be imperilled. In a state with ten thousand chariots, the one who assassinates his lord will be from a family with a thousand chariots; in a state with a thousand chariots, the one who assassinates his lord will be from a family of a hundred chariots. To have one thousand in ten thousand, or one hundred in one thousand, is not an inconsiderable [share],[27] but if one were to put righteousness last and profit first, they would not be satiated without snatching more. There has never been one with humanity who yet abandoned his family; there has never been one with righteousness who yet placed his lord last [i.e. in his list of obligations]. Surely Your Majesty should say: 'Humanity and righteousness, and nothing more!' Why must you speak of profit?"   (*Mencius* 1A.1)

When one considers that King Hui may well have been older than Mencius, yet still addresses him honorifically as "venerable man", one can imagine his surprise when Mencius takes him to task for what he presumably intended as a harmless formulaic greeting. But Mencius does not allow misconceptions about the purpose of government, even for the sake of courteous rhetoric. Government is about spreading humanity and righteousness; it is not about profit-seeking. To the familiar Confucian affirmations of moral governance, Mencius adds a parallel argument: it is prudent.[28] As before, the assumption is that ordinary people will follow the lead set by their superiors, and if the king himself makes profit-seeking his principle of government, his subjects are sure to imitate him, with hazardous consequences.[29] Who has the most to lose in a society devoted to profit-seeking, if not the king himself? Humanity and righteousness are useful virtues because a populace that has imbibed these virtues will not depose its sovereign.

Mencius probably did not intend this appeal to prudence as dispositive, but he did not underestimate its value in persuasion. Compare *Mencius* 6B.4, where Mencius objects to Song Keng 宋牼 (also called Song Xing 宋鈃), a philosopher of uncertain affiliation who intended to persuade the kings of Qin 秦 and Chu to end their war because it would be profitable to do so. The language is very similar to that of 1A.1:

> [Mencius] said: "Sir, your aspiration is great, but your slogan is unacceptable. If you persuade the kings of Qin and Chu by means of profit, they will recall the captains of their threefold armies because they are delighted by profit; then the men-at-arms in the threefold armies will be pleased by the ceasefire, and will be delighted by profit. If you cause ministers to serve their lords by embracing profit, if you cause sons to serve their fathers by embracing profit, if you cause younger brothers to serve their elder brothers by embracing profit, then lords and ministers, fathers and sons, and elder brothers and younger brothers will abandon humanity and righteousness and receive one another by embracing profit. There has never been [a ruler] in such a case who did not perish. Sir, if you persuade the kings of Qin and Chu by means of humanity and righteousness, they will recall the captains of their threefold armies because they are delighted by humanity and righteousness; then the men-at-arms in the threefold armies will be pleased by the ceasefire and delight in humanity and righteousness. If you cause ministers to serve their lords by embracing humanity and righteousness, if you cause sons to serve their fathers by embracing humanity and righteousness, if you cause younger brothers to serve their elder brothers by embracing humanity and righteousness, then lords and ministers, fathers and sons, and elder brothers and younger brothers will abandon profit-seeking and receive one another by embracing humanity and righteousness. There has never been [a ruler] in such a case who did not become a true king. Why must you speak of 'profit'?"

In some respects, however, Mencius differed from Confucius. Whereas Confucius was content to let people die of famine, if necessary, in order to preserve trustworthy government (*Analects* 12.7),

Mencius held that rulers need to promote the people's material welfare to a certain minimum standard before moral suasion can be practicable:

> [Mencius] said: "Only a gentleman can have a constant heart without constant sustenance. In the case of the populace, if they have no constant sustenance, they will accordingly have no constant heart. And if they have no constant heart, they will indulge themselves and veer into intemperance; there is nothing that they would not do. To pursue and punish them after they have fallen into crime would be to ensnare the people. How could a humane man in [the ruler's] position ensnare the people? For this reason, in determining the sustenance of the people, an enlightened lord must cause them, on the one hand, to have enough to serve their father and mother, and, on the other hand, to have enough to support their wives and children, so that in happy years they are always full, and in inauspicious years they escape untimely death. Only then do you drive them towards goodness, so that the people find it easy to follow you." (*Mencius* 1A.7)[30]

Without abandoning the characteristic Confucian concern for moral self-cultivation, Mencius evidently believed that it was ineffective to preach to the people about morality as long as they were routinely starved and mactated.

Lastly, a point that has been frequently miscast by modern readers who wish to portray Mencius as a kind of proto-democrat:[31] whereas Confucius had relatively little to say about the legitimation of rulers – a legitimate ruler is simply one who acts as a ruler should – Mencius had an intricate theory of Heaven's Mandate that also explained why succession did not always proceed from father to son:[32]

> [The disciple] Wan Zhang 萬章 said: "Yao gave the world to Shun – is this the case?"

> Mencius said: "No, the Son of Heaven cannot give the world to another person".
>
> "Then if Shun possessed the world, who gave it to him?"
>
> [Mencius] said: "Heaven gave it to him." (*Mencius* 5A.5)

Yao was a sage king who abdicated and handed over the throne to the virtuous commoner Shun, rather than to his own son. But in Mencius's view, Yao did not have the authority to make such a transfer himself; rather, it took place because Heaven sanctioned it. For the ruler does not possess his own kingdom; he is only stewarding it for the true owner, Heaven. Mencius elaborates: "Heaven does not speak, but merely reveals itself through actions and affairs." The Son of Heaven may recommend a worthy successor, but this candidate will not become the next Son of Heaven unless Heaven endorses him with unambiguous signs.

> [Mencius] said: "If you place him in charge of sacrifices and the hundred spirits enjoy them, this means that Heaven has accepted him. If you place him in charge of [terrestrial] affairs and the affairs are all orderly, if the Hundred Surnames are at peace with him, this means that the people have accepted him. Heaven gave him [the demesne] and the people gave it to him too; thus I have said: 'The Son of Heaven cannot give the world to another person.'" (*Mencius* 5A.5)

Although Mencius frequently reminds his interlocutors, as in the above passage, that a ruler's legitimacy is revealed through the approval of the people, failing to perceive that the approval of Heaven is always the true determinant would lead to grave misunderstandings – as in the next section, where Wan Zhang asks why abdication has gone out of favour as a method of royal succession:

> Wan Zhang asked: "People have a saying, 'In the time of Yu 禹, virtue decayed [as compared to Yao and Shun], for he did not transmit [the throne] to a worthy man, but transmitted it to his son.' Is this the case?"

Mencius said: "It is not so. If Heaven gives it to a worthy man, it will be given to a worthy man; if Heaven gives it to [the ruler's] son, it will be given to his son."

(*Mencius* 5A.6)

Once again, Heaven's choice is discernible through the aggregate actions of the populace. As the passage goes on to relate, when Yu died, the people spontaneously paid homage to his capable son, Qi 啓, and not to the successor that Yu himself recommended, a worthy named Yi 益. As the first competent prince in several generations, Qi was not an unwise choice for the people to follow. But it is still necessary to distinguish the roles of Heaven and of the people on a theoretical level, even if there are no cases in the *Mencius* where Heaven explicitly overruled the manifest will of the people. For a shortsighted or deluded populace may try to install a defective government that Heaven cannot ordain. Mencius would never contend that Heaven's hand would be forced in such an instance. On the contrary, he took pains to explain that Heaven's will lay behind all these developments:

That Shun, Yu, and Yi served as ministers for differing periods, and that the sons [of Yao, Shun, and Yu] were of differing worth – this was all due to Heaven. It was not something that was done by human beings. When something is done though no one does it, it is due to Heaven; if something comes about though no one brings it about, it is due to the Mandate. (*Mencius* 5A.6)

The unstated elements of Mencius's argument are at least as important as the explicit ones; for no one in Warring States times could pretend that all crown princes were as capable as Yu's formidable son Qi. Any critical reader would have to ask why Heaven permits petty and inept rulers to accede to the throne. In effect, Mencius is saying that succession from father to son is the norm in his day *because Heaven wills it*. If Heaven willed another method, such as abdication, it would approve instances of it, but – as the disastrous episode involving Zizhi 子之 and King Zikuai of Yan 燕王子噲 demonstrated (*Mencius* 2B.8) – Heaven no longer affirms abdication. Abdication may have been viable in the past, but in the present it is mere folly.[33]

In accordance with his theory of Heaven's Mandate, Mencius distinguishes between the hegemon (*ba* 霸), or a warlord who rules by strength, and the true king (*wang* 王), or the Son of Heaven who attains the genuine submission of the people by conquering their hearts:[34]

> Mencius said: "One who uses force and stints on humanity is a hegemon, but a hegemon must have a large state; one who uses virtue to carry out humanity is a true king, and a true king need not depend on a large [domain]. [The Sage-King] Tang [became a king] with only seventy square *li*, King Wen with only a hundred. When one makes people submit by force, one does not make them submit in their hearts; [they do so because] their own force is insufficient. When one makes people submit through virtue, they are delighted in their innermost hearts and truly submit, as the seventy disciples submitted to Confucius. When it is said in the *Odes*, 'From the West, from the East, from the South, from the North – ah, there was none who did not submit,'[35] this is what it refers to."
>
> (*Mencius* 2A.3)

No one faced with a choice of submitting to a virtuous king or defending a coercive despot will ever choose the latter:

> Thus it is said: "One does not confine the people with boundaries such as demarcated frontiers; one does not safeguard the state with escarpments of mountains and valleys; one does not overawe the world with the keenness of one's weapons and armour. One who has attained the Way will have many helpers; one who has lost the Way will have few helpers. The ultimate of having few helpers is to be betrayed by one's own kin; the ultimate of having many helpers is to be obeyed by the whole world. [A true king attacking a

tyrant] will be one who is obeyed by the whole world attacking one who is betrayed by his own kin. Thus although there are times when the noble man does not fight, he is sure to win when he does." (*Mencius* 2B.1)[36]

In an interview with Lord Wen of Teng 滕文公 (fl. 326 BCE), however, Mencius is forced to concede that, in certain extreme situations, even a policy of pure morality cannot save a state from extinction. Wedged between the mighty states of Qi and Chu, Teng has little hope of survival, and Mencius thus counsels the beleaguered Lord Wen to act as a beacon to later generations:

> Lord Wen of Teng said: "The men of Qi are about to fortify Xue. I am very fearful; how would it be right to proceed?"
>
> Mencius responded: "In the past, King Tai [the grandfather of King Wen and thus the ancestor of the House of Zhou] dwelled in Bin. The men of Di invaded [Bin], so he left it and dwelled beneath Mount Qi. It was not that he chose to do this, but he had no alternative. If you do good, there will surely be a king among the sons and grandsons of your progeny. In commencing an enterprise, a noble man suspends a thread that can be continued. Whether he attains success is up to Heaven. My lord, what can you do about [the men of Qi]? You may do no more than exert yourself to do good." (*Mencius* 1B.14)

Because it is Heaven, not man, who disposes, most of us do not have an opportunity to become true kings. Lord Wen may be doomed, but not his line: if he leaves behind an admirable example, he may yet serve as an inspiration to unborn kings of the future. King Tai himself, after all, was not really a king; we call him "king" because he was a progenitor of kings.

FOUR

Xunzi

With Xunzi, we come to a thinker unlike any that we have encountered before. Most apparently to Western readers, Xunzi, unlike Confucius or Mencius, has no Latinized name – a direct reflection of the fact that when the Jesuits arrived in China and began to study Confucianism, Xunzi had already been repudiated by Chinese scholasticism as at best an imperfect Confucian, and certainly not a member of the *daotong* 道統 ("genealogy of the Way"), the term for the orthodox tradition stretching back to the sages.

Xunzi's prestige has, correspondingly, reached extreme highs and lows over the centuries. In his own day, he was revered as "the most senior of the masters" (*zui wei lao shi* 最爲老師),[1] and numbered among his students some of the most influential men in the Chinese world, including Han Fei 韓非 (d. 233 BCE) and Li Si 李斯 (d. 208 BCE). He was still widely celebrated in the Western Han dynasty, when Dong Zhongshu 董仲舒 (fl. 152–119 BCE), one of the leading intellectual figures, is reported to have written a paean to him (now lost).[2] But by Eastern Han times, Mencius – construed throughout Chinese history as Xunzi's nemesis – had eclipsed him in the minds of most literati.[3]

Thus the first three or four centuries after Xunzi's death witnessed a slow but continuous decline in his reputation. Thereafter the pace of this decline quickened. By the Tang 唐 dynasty, even literati who admired Xunzi – such as Han Yu 韓愈 (768–824)[4] – were careful to add that his works contain grave mistakes. In the Song 宋, there were still some voices that praised him, but the opinion with the greatest long-term consequences was that of Zhu Xi 朱熹 (1130–1200), who declared that Xunzi's philosophy resembled that of non-Confucians such as Shen Buhai 申不害 (fl. 354–340 BCE) and Shang Yang 商鞅 (d. 338 BCE), and that he was indirectly responsible for the notorious disasters of the Qin dynasty.[5] For the rest of imperial history,[6] Xunzi was rejected by the cultural mainstream; into the twentieth century, he was criticized by intellectuals such as Kang Youwei 康有爲 (1858–1927),[7] Tan Sitong 譚嗣同 (1865–1898),[8] and Liang Qichao 梁啟超 (1873–1929)[9] as the progenitor of the Confucian scriptural legacy, which, in their view, had derailed the original Confucian mission and plunged China into a cycle of authoritarianism and corruption that lasted for more than two thousand years.

Today the tide has turned almost completely. Xunzi is one of the most popular philosophers throughout East Asia,[10] and has been the subject of more books published in English over the past two decades than any other Chinese philosopher, vastly outstripping Mencius.[11] From a twenty-first-century perspective, this revival of interest in Xunzi is not hard to explain: his body of work has always been one of the best preserved, and with the commonplace scholastic objection to his philosophy – namely, that he was wrong to say human nature is evil (*xing e* 性惡) – having lost most of its cogency, it is only to be expected that philosophical readers should be attracted to his creative but rigorous arguments. In this sense one could say that Xunzi has finally been restored, more than two millennia after his death, to his erstwhile position as "the most senior of the masters".[12] For he is probably the most complex philosopher that China has ever produced – and not coincidentally one of the most controversial.

Another conspicuous difference: whereas Confucius and Mencius did not pen the books that we now use to reconstruct their philosophies, the bulk of the *Xunzi* consists of essays that were unquestionably written by Xunzi himself. There are a few chapters that could not have been written by Xunzi – at least not in their present form – because they call Xunzi by the title Sun Qingzi 孫卿子, "Master

Chamberlain Sun",[13] which he himself would not have used. But, as we shall see, whoever is responsible for these documents was intimately familiar with Xunzi's philosophy and did not misrepresent it. The received text of the *Xunzi* was compiled by the bibliographer Liu Xiang 劉向 (79–78 BCE) out of various independently circulating documents,[14] but the chapters fit together so seamlessly that Xunzi could only have imagined his work as a coherent *oeuvre*. Xunzi did not envision himself as a teacher whose sphere was limited to direct contact with his disciples; rather, he represented a new breed of thinker, one who aimed, through writing, to influence diverse classes of readers across the land, most of whom he would never meet.[15] In Xunzi's book, the synthetic format and presentation of ideas reflect, like the ideas themselves, the revolutionary intellectual developments of the third century BCE.

The most crucial difference of all, finally, is that whereas Confucius and Mencius made only the barest statements about the nature of the cosmos, and did not by any means consider the study of cosmology to be indispensable to moral self-cultivation, Xunzi had a robust theory of the universe and its relation to moral philosophy. Indeed, Xunzi considered morality impossible without an understanding of the patterns of the cosmos. But before we can appreciate this aspect of Xunzi's philosophy, we must visit the intellectual cul-de-sac that sadly dominated most discussions of Xunzi in imperial China: his theory that *xing* is evil.[16]

In practice, Xunzi's claim that *xing* is evil means that following the impulses of one's *xing*, without reflecting on them and moderating them, will lead one to evil acts.[17] It should be emphasized that *e*, the Chinese word translated here as "evil", is not to be understood in the Christian sense of "diabolical" or "antithetical to God". The basic meaning of *e* is "detestable" (its verbal cognate, *wu* 惡, means "to hate"), but in classical Chinese it is the ordinary antonym of *shan* 善, the word used by Mencius for "good". In Xunzi, *e* refers to human nature in its unremediated – and hence harmful – state.

Mencius, we remember, had argued that *xing* is good, but this did not mean that people are all necessarily good; rather, it meant that we all have the capacity to become good, but that some people develop this capacity and others do not. Xunzi arrived at a similar point of view, but with diametrically opposed rhetoric:

> Mencius said: "Since one can learn, one's *xing* is good." This is not so. This [point of view] does not attain to knowledge of human *xing* and does not investigate the distinction between *xing* and artifice. *Xing* is what is spontaneous from Heaven, what cannot be learned, what cannot be acquired. Ritual and morality arise from the sages. People become capable of them through learning; they perfect themselves by acquiring them. What cannot be learned, what cannot be acquired, and is in human beings, is called *xing*. What is in human beings that they can become capable of through learning, and that they can acquire to perfect themselves, is called "artifice". This is the distinction between *xing* and artifice. (*Xunzi* 23.1c)[18]

> Mencius said: "Human *xing* is good." I say: This is not so. From ancient times until the present, all that has been called "good" in the world is rectitude, principle, peace and order. What is called "evil" is partiality, malice, rebelliousness and disorder. This is the distinction between good and evil. Now can one sincerely believe that human *xing* is originally upright, principled, peaceful and orderly? Then what use for the sage kings, what use for ritual and morality? (*Xunzi* 23.3a)

The major difference between Mencius and Xunzi is not that they held incompatible theories of human nature, but that they used the term *xing* in fundamentally dissimilar senses. Whereas Mencius used *xing* to refer to the ideal state that an organism can be expected to attain given the right nurturing conditions, Xunzi operated with a more traditional definition: "What is so by birth is called *xing*" (*Xunzi* 22.1b).[19] Since ritual and morality are manifestly not inborn, they cannot be reckoned as *xing*; rather, in Xunzi's parlance, they are *wei* 僞, "artifice". Thus *xing* refers to the basic faculties, capacities and desires that we have from birth, "artifice" to all the traits that we acquire through our own conscious actions. And if we achieve any goodness, it must be because of our artifice:

> Human *xing* is evil; what is good is artifice. Now human *xing* is as follows. At birth there is fondness for profit in it. If one goes along with this, contention and robbery arise, and deference and courtesy are thereby destroyed. At birth there is envy and hatred in it. If one goes along with this, violence and banditry arise, and loyalty and trust are thereby destroyed. At birth there are the desires of the ear and eye: there is fondness for sound and colour in them. If one goes along with this, perversion and disorder arise, and ritual, morality, refinement and principles are thereby destroyed. This being the case, by obeying one's *xing* and going along with one's emotions, one must set forth in robbery and contention, accord with the violation of [social] division and disruption of the natural order, and come home to turmoil. Thus there must be the transformation [brought about by] the methods of a teacher and the Way of ritual and morality; only then will one set forth in deference and courtesy, accord with refinement and principles, and come home to order. Using these [considerations] to see it, human *xing* is clearly evil; what is good is artifice.
>
> (*Xunzi* 23.1a)

At the same time, since everyone is born with the same *xing* – we all have the same sense organs, and, as we shall see, the same mental faculties – it stands to reason that the path to moral perfection is open to anyone. And thus Xunzi repeats Mencius's assertion that even a beggar in the street can become a sage, as long as he is willing to put forth the effort:

> A sage is a person who has attained [sagehood] through accumulation [of learning]. It was asked: Sagehood can be achieved by accumulating [learning], but not all of us do –

why is this? I answered: We can, but we cannot be forced. Thus a small man could become a noble man, but is not willing to do so. A noble man could become a small man, but is not willing to do so. Small man, noble man – it is never the case that one cannot become the other. The [reason that] the one does not become the other is not that he cannot, but that he cannot be forced. This is how a person in the street can become Yu. (*Xunzi* 23.5b)[20]

Not much of Xunzi's essay on *xing*, it should be emphasized, can be said to refute Mencius's position. The two thinkers arrived, in fact, at remarkably similar points of view. Both would have agreed that people can perfect themselves and that such an achievement requires great exertion and self-motivation. And both would have agreed that without lifelong practice of self-cultivation, people are evil. These similarities have led some commentators to suggest that Xunzi's objections "are not quite to the point".[21] What prompted Xunzi to dissent from Mencius's characterization of *xing* as good if his own theory was to be so difficult to distinguish from the one that he criticized?

The question is crucial, for as long as Xunzi's philosophy is reduced to the tenet that *xing* is evil, one cannot appreciate how he went beyond his predecessors – and readers of later centuries, who seemed not to peruse much of Xunzi beyond Chapter 23, were able to dismiss him all too easily. While it is impossible for us today to be sure of Xunzi's argumentative motivations, my sense is that Xunzi wished to highlight his conviction that the proper models for moral behaviour lie outside the self, which is fundamentally opposed to a Mencian notion of Four Beginnings lodged within the human heart. Whereas Mencians have always emphasized looking inwards for moral direction – sometimes complicated, as we shall see in the next chapter, by their acknowledgement that the heart can be corrupted – self-cultivation in the Xunzian style is inconceivable without looking *outwards*.

Xunzi held that, for most ordinary people, the best guide is the set of rituals handed down by the sages. ("Ritual and morality arise from the sages", we remember.) And what are these rituals? Western scholarship has understandably lavished attention on Xunzian statements about ritual that would seem to invite a comparison with modern contractarianism, but the inadequacy of this line of analysis will soon become clear. In the most famous of these passages, Xunzi attributes, in a manner reminiscent of Hobbes or Rousseau, the genesis of the rituals to the sages' recognition that unbridled competition produces an unsustainable situation for all:

> Whence did rituals arise? I say: One is born with desires; if one desires and does not obtain [the object of one's desires], then one cannot but seek it. If, in seeking, people have no measures or limits, then there cannot but be contention. Contention makes disorder, and disorder privation. The Former Kings hated such disorder, and established ritual and morality in order to divide [the people into classes], in order to nourish people's desires and grant what people seek. They brought it about that desires need not be deprived of objects, that objects need not be depleted by desires; the two support each other and grow. This is where rituals arise.
> (*Xunzi* 19.1a)

This is the opening of Xunzi's famous "Discourse on Ritual" ("Lilun" 禮論), and similar statements are found in other chapters:

> To be honoured as the Son of Heaven and richly to possess the world – this is the common desire of humans [by virtue of their] essence. But if people follow their desires, then boundaries cannot contain them and objects cannot satisfy them. Thus the Former Kings restrained them and established for them ritual and morality in order to divide them [into classes].
> (*Xunzi* 4.12)

To judge from such pronouncements, "ritual" might seem like no more than a shorthand name for the nexus of regulations that allow humankind to enjoy nature's bounty harmoniously.[22] With rituals in place, "desires need not be deprived of objects, that objects need not be depleted by desires". Replace "rituals" with "contracts" (or the like), and Xunzi would seem to emerge as a shining contractarian. We all have desires, and were we to go about satisfying them in a lawless world, the result would be only unrequited desire. The prospect of such chaos is resolved through ritual: with the establishment of a few ground rules, we can fulfil our desires, at least to a level of self-sufficiency, without being unduly impeded by others in our midst.

But there is more to Xunzi's theory of ritual than this. The necessary rituals, in his view, must institute ranks and distinctions in society, for without them harmony cannot be achieved (*Xunzi* 9.3). All people have their place, like the hairs in his famous figure of the fur collar (*Xunzi* 1.11). Social organization – which, for Xunzi, always means social stratification – is the method by which human beings, despite their paltry physical gifts, are able to dominate all other forms of life:

> Water and fire have *qi* but no life; grasses and trees have life but no awareness; birds and beasts have awareness but no morality. Human beings have breath and life and awareness, and they have morality in addition. Thus they are the most noble [beings] in the world. They do not have the strength of an ox, nor do they run like a horse, but oxen and horses are used by them. Why is this? I say: People can form societies; [animals] cannot form societies. How can people form societies? Through division [of labour]. How can division proceed? I say: morality. Thus division with morality brings about harmony. (*Xunzi* 9.16a)

The reference at the end to morality suggests two reasons why a contractarian reading of Xunzi fails to capture all the nuances of his theory. First, Xunzi elsewhere explicitly denies that an arbitrarily chosen set of rituals would be effective. Rather, the rituals of the sage kings are legitimate because they accord with human nature; by implication, any competing ritual code would necessarily fail:[23]

What is it that makes humans human? I say: their making of distinctions. Desiring food when hungry, desiring warmth when cold, desiring respite when toiling, liking profit and disliking harm – these [characteristics] are all possessed by people from birth. They are what is immediately so. This is the similarity between [the sage] Yu and [the tyrant] Jie 桀. This being the case, what makes humans human is not specifically that they have two feet and no pelt [or plumage – i.e. that humans are featherless bipeds]. It is their making of distinctions. Now the *xingxing* [a legendary ape with no hair] resembles us, and also has two feet and no pelt. But the noble man sips his soup and eats his food cooked. Thus what makes humans human is not specifically that they have two feet and no pelt. It is their making of distinctions. Birds and beasts have fathers and sons, but no intimacy between fathers and sons. They have males and females, but no separation between man and woman. Thus the Way of Humans is nothing other than to make distinctions. There are no greater distinctions than social distinctions. There are no greater social distinctions than the rituals. There are no greater rituals than those of the Sage Kings.   (*Xunzi* 5.4)[24]

Xunzi's argument here brings us to territory that Mencius never broached. He claims that human beings, unlike any other species of animal, make certain distinctions and live by them: male is distinguished from female, old from young, and so on – and it is altogether natural that we do so. That is the Way. The rituals of the sage kings identify the natural order and augment it by confirming the distinctions that we are bound to make by nature. And just as there is only one Way (more on this presently), there can be only one proper set of rituals. The sage kings apprehended it, and their rituals embody it. Modern contractarians do not, as a rule, postulate that workable social rules must have this kind of cosmological underpinning.

The second reason why Xunzi cannot be adequately understood as a contractarian is that rituals, in his conception, not only facilitate social cohesion, but also foster psychological development. Indeed, if they did not, they would be mere instruments of expedience, not rituals. These dimensions become clear when Xunzi begins to discuss specific rituals and their purposes:

> Thus serving the living without loyal generosity or reverent formality is called uncivil; sending off the dead without loyal generosity or reverent formality is called miserly. The noble man condemns incivility and is ashamed of miserliness; thus the inner and outer coffins consist of seven layers for the Son of Heaven, five layers for a feudal lord, three layers for a grand master, and two layers for a man-of-service. Thereafter, in order to revere and adorn them, there are for each [rank] protocols regarding the quantity and richness of [mortuary] robes and foodstuffs, and grades for the [corresponding] flabellum and décor. This causes life and death, ending and beginning, to be [treated] as one, and people's yearnings to be satiated. This is the Way of the Former Kings, the ridgepole of the loyal minister and filial son.
>
> (*Xunzi* 19.4a–b)

We observe sumptuary regulations, in other words, in order to learn how to avoid incivility and miserliness. Elsewhere in the same chapter, Xunzi discusses the purpose of the mandatory three-year mourning period for deceased rulers and parents (which, in practice, lasts only until the twenty-fifth month – that is, the first month of the third year) and explains that, here too, the rituals have a moral purpose: they help us conduct ourselves properly by providing suitable forms for us to express emotions that are so deep as to be potentially debilitating.

> When a wound is colossal, its duration is long; when pain is profound, the recovery is slow. The three-year mourning period is a form established with reference to emotions; it is the means by which one conveys the acme of one's pain. The untrimmed sackcloth garment, the [hatband and waistband] of the female nettle plant, the staff,[25] the hut where

one dwells, the gruel that one eats, the brushwood that one uses as a mat and clod of earth that one uses as a pillow – by these means, one conveys the acme of one's pain. The three-year mourning period ends with the twenty-fifth month; one's pain of grief is not yet exhausted, nor have pining and longing yet departed from one's heart, but the rituals cut off [the mourning period] here because there is an endpoint to sending off the dead and a period [after which] one must return to the living. ...   (*Xunzi* 19.9a)

Shall we follow those foolish, rude, licentious and perverse people who forget by the evening those who have died in the morning? If we were to allow this, we would not even be the equals of birds and beasts. How could we dwell without disorder in the same society as such people? Or shall we follow cultivated and refined gentlemen, for whom the three-year mourning period, ending with the twenty-fifth month, passes as swiftly as a team of four horses [glimpsed through] a crack in a wall? If we were to go along with them, [the mourning period] would be interminable. Thus the Former Kings and Sages accordingly determined the [right] period by establishing the midpoint. Once [mourning] has become sufficient to attain a due form and pattern, it is set aside.
                                   (*Xunzi* 19.9c)

Xunzi's discussion of the village wine-drinking ceremony (*xiang* 鄉), similarly, goes through the rite *in extenso*, showing how each element bespeaks an underlying moral principle. For example, the fact that the host fetches the guest of honour himself, but expects the other guests to arrive on their own, underscores the distinctions that need to be drawn between noble and base. And the detail that each participant toasts the next, serially and according to their ages, demonstrates that one can align society according to seniority without excluding anybody. When the guest of honour retires, the host bows and escorts him out, and the formal occasion comes to an end: this is to make it known that one can feast at leisure without becoming disorderly. The clear implication is that by taking part in the rite, we can gradually comprehend the moral principles that the sages wished us to embody (*Xunzi* 20.5).

Xunzi's rituals have such an important role to play in our emotional and moral development that he spends an entire chapter limning what are essentially rituals of artistic expression. The term he uses is "music" (*yue* 樂), which is not identical to ritual, but Xunzi's conception of their origin and purpose is so similar that one can scarcely speak of one without the other. Thus "ritual and music" (*liyue* 禮樂) can only be understood as two aspects of human artifice: "ritual" refers to forms that affect social cohesion, "music" to those involving the orderly expression of human emotions. But the crucial point is that the sages created both.

> Music is joy; it is what human emotions cannot avoid. Thus humans cannot be without music. If we are joyous, then we must express it in sounds and tones and give form to it in movement and quietude. And the Way of Humanity is fulfilled in sounds and tones, in movement and quietude, and in the changes in the techniques of the *xing*.[26] Thus humans cannot be without joy, and joy cannot be without form, but if that form is not [in line with] the Way, then there cannot but be disorder. The Former Kings hated this disorder; thus they instituted the sounds of the Odes and Hymns in order to make them accord with the Way. They brought it about that their sounds were sufficient [to give form] to joy but were not dissipated; they brought it about that their patterned [compositions] were sufficient to make distinctions but were not timorous [?];[27] they brought it about that the directness, complexity, richness, and rhythm were sufficient to move people's good minds; they brought it about that heterodox and impure *qi* would have no opportunity to attach itself. (*Xunzi* 20.1)

Like all Confucians, Xunzi accepts that human beings have certain irrepressible impulses, and does not contend that they are objectionable in themselves. The problem is that unreflective outbursts driven solely by our emotional responses may cause harm, and thus we are enjoined to be mindful of our impulses, rather than to extinguish them.[28] To aid us in this process, the sages left behind appropriate musical forms that we can use to channel our need to express ourselves. That is to say, everyone feels a need to sing or dance at some point, and it would be folly to suppress these urges, but the danger is that we might begin to sing disruptive songs such as "Let's Plant in the Autumn and Harvest in the Spring", whose influence could be harmful to an agrarian society. In order to keep us from spontaneously intoning such destructive songs, the sages gave us wholesome songs to sing instead – such as, to continue the example, the "Let's Plant in the Spring and Harvest in the Autumn" song. What Xunzi meant by this corpus of songs, of course, is the canonical collection of *Odes* that all Confucians seem to have regarded as a nonpareil repository of edifying literature.[29]

Xunzi's immediate purpose in this section was to counter the Mohist view that music is wasteful. We remember from Mencius's discussion with King Xuan of Qi that the ruler's lavish musical productions provoked resentment among the populace (because they were prevented from enjoying them), and Mo Di expanded on what must have been widespread popular outrage to argue that music itself is unjustifiable in moral society. Xunzi countered that by focusing exclusively on the material costs, Mo Di and his followers failed to recognize the psychological utility of music as an instrument of moral suasion.[30]

> Sounds and music enter people deeply; they transform people quickly. Thus the Former Kings were careful to make [music] patterned. When music is centred and balanced, the people are harmonious and not dissipated. When music is stern and grave, the people are uniform and not disorderly. When the people are harmonious and uniform, the army is firm and the citadels secure; enemy states dare not invade. When this is the case, then none among the Hundred Clans are not at peace in their dwellings; all are joyous in the

neighbourhoods and fully satisfied with their superiors. Only then will the name and repute [of the ruler of such a state] be shining and his glory great; within the Four Seas, none among the people will be unwilling to accept him as their teacher. This is the beginning of kingship. When music is overwrought and seduces us to malice, then the people are dissipated, indolent, crude and base. Dissipation and indolence lead to disorder, crudity and baseness to contention. When there is disorder and contention, the army is soft and the citadels pillaged; enemies will threaten [such a state]. When this is the case, the Hundred Clans are not at peace in their dwellings; they are not joyous in their neighbourhoods or satisfied with their superiors. Thus when rituals and music lapse, and heterodox tones arise, this is the root of territorial encroachment, humiliation and disgrace. Thus the Former Kings took ritual and music to be noble and heterodox tones to be base. This [principle] appears in the "Procedures of the Officials":[31] "The affairs of the Grand Music-Master are: to cultivate the edicts and commands; to investigate poetic stanzas; to proscribe licentious sounds – so that [the people] act in accord with the seasons, and barbarous customs and heterodox tones dare not bring disorder upon the 'Elegantiae'."[32]   (*Xunzi* 20.2)

Thus ritual-and-music is, for Xunzi as for Confucius, a mode of moral self-cultivation, but his underlying cosmology is radically different. Confucius had nothing to say about the origin of the rituals; they were but a cultural given that one is required to attune and adjust, with sincere moral consciousness, as circumstances demand. And this practice, in Confucius's view, trains us in the discipline of moral reasoning that is necessary to lead a respectable life. For Xunzi too, practising the rituals propels our moral development, but not because we are supposed to alter them to suit varying conditions; rather, the rituals are the practicable code that the sages, who penetrated the fundamental patterns of the cosmos, left behind for the benefit of their less-talented posterity:

Those who have forded a river mark the deep spots; if the markers are not clear, one will stumble. Those who have brought order to the people mark the Way; if the markers are not clear, there will be disorder. The rituals are the markers; to oppose the rituals is to blind the world; to blind the world is a great disorder. Thus if nothing is left unclear about the Way, there are different markers for the outer and inner, and a constancy pertaining to the hidden and the manifest, the people will stumble no more.   (*Xunzi* 17.11)

What Xunzi meant by this "constancy" is a relatively new concept to Confucianism: the Way (*dao* 道).[33] Confucius and Mencius had used this term, but never with any necessary cosmological connotations; for earlier Confucians, *dao* simply referred to "the right path". Thus when Confucius said "If one hears the Way in the morning, it is acceptable to die in the evening" (*Analects* 4.8), he was not talking about apprehending the basic structure of the universe. "The Way" was no more than "the right way to act".[34] Xunzi, who lived after such texts as the *Laozi* 老子 had gained currency among the reading public, turned the Way into something more complex.

There is a constancy to Heaven's processes. It is not preserved by Yao and it does not perish because of Jie. To respond to it with the right pattern is auspicious; to respond to it with disorder is inauspicious. If you strengthen the base and spend in moderation, Heaven cannot impoverish you. If the nourishment [of the people] is achieved and your movements are in accordance with the seasons, Heaven cannot cause you to be ill. If you cultivate the Way and are not of two [minds], Heaven cannot ruin you. Thus floods and drought cannot bring about famine and thirst; cold and heat cannot bring about disease; portents and wonders cannot bring about inauspiciousness. But if the base is neglected and expenditures are extravagant, Heaven cannot enrich you. If the nourishment [of the people] is desultory and your movements are irregular, Heaven cannot cause you to be hale. If you turn your back on the Way and act thought-lessly, Heaven cannot bring about auspiciousness. Thus there will be famine even without floods or drought, disease even without cold or heat, inauspiciousness even without portents and wonders. The seasons will be received just as in an orderly age, but your calamities and ruination will be different from [the bounty of] an orderly age. You cannot complain to Heaven, for its Way is such.[35]   (*Xunzi* 17.1)

When a ruler governs a state well, there are bound to be good results; when a ruler governs a state badly, there are bound to be bad results. Disasters can have no long-term consequences because a well-governed state will prosper even in the face of disasters, and a poorly governed state will be vanquished even if it avoids disasters altogether. (Xunzi's opinion of Hurricane Katrina would undoubtedly have been that hurricanes strike all states equally, but a well-governed state will be prepared for such an event, whereas a poorly governed state will be in no position to respond to the crisis.) Consequently, Heaven plays a sure but indirect role in determining out fortune or misfortune. Heaven never intercedes directly in human affairs, but human affairs are certain to succeed or fail according to a timeless pattern that Heaven determined before human beings existed.

Are order and disorder in Heaven? I say: The revolutions of the sun, moon, and stars, and the cyclical calendar – these were the same under Yu and Jie. Since Yu brought about order and Jie disorder, order and disorder are not in Heaven. And the seasons? I say: Luxuriantly, [vegetation] begins to bloom and grow in spring and summer; crops are harvested and stored in autumn and winter. This, too, was the same under Yu and Jie. Since Yu brought about order and Jie disorder, order and disorder are not in the seasons.   (*Xunzi* 17.4)

If we attempt to conduct ourselves or our society in a manner that is incompatible with "the constancy", we will suffer – and have only ourselves to blame.

Heaven does not stop winter because people dislike cold; Earth does not stop its expansiveness because people dislike great distances; the noble man does not stop his right conduct because petty men rant and rave. Heaven has a constant Way; Earth has its constant dimensions; the noble man has a constant bearing. (*Xunzi* 17.5)

At this juncture Xunzi makes a crucial distinction between knowing Heaven and knowing its Way. The former is impossible, and therefore a waste of time to attempt, but the latter is open to all who try. To cite a modern parallel, it is not difficult to understand *how* the force of gravity works by carefully observing its effects in the phenomenal world, but to understand *why* gravity works is a different matter altogether. Xunzi would say that one should constrain one's enquiries to learning how gravity works, and then think about how to apply this irresistible force of nature to improve the lives of humankind. His attitude was not scientific in our sense.

Thus one who is enlightened about the distinction between Heaven and man can be called an Ultimate Person (*zhiren* 至人).[36] What is completed without any action, what is attained without being sought – this is called the agency of Heaven. Therefore, however profound they may be, such people do not add their reasoning to it; however great they may be, they do not add their abilities to it; however perceptive they may be, they do not add their investigations to it. This is what is called not competing with the agency of Heaven. … Their aspiration with respect to Heaven is no more than to observe the phenomena that can be taken as regular periods [e.g. the progression of the seasons or stars]. Their aspiration with respect to Earth is no more than to observe the matters that yield [i.e. crops]. Their aspiration with respect to the four seasons is no more than to observe the data that can be made to serve [humanity]. Their aspiration with respect to *yin* and *yang* [i.e. the two component aspects of *qi*] is no more than to observe their harmonious [interactions] that can bring about order.

(*Xunzi* 17.2a–3b)

In a moment of poetic exuberance, Xunzi concludes:

> To extol Heaven and long for it –
> how does that compare to domesticating its creatures and controlling them?
> To follow Heaven and sing paeans to it –
> how does that compare to handling Heaven's Mandate and making use of it?
> To gaze at the seasons and await them –
> how does that compare to responding to the seasons and employing them?
> To accord with things and let them reproduce [at their own pace] –
> how does that compare to unleashing one's ability and transforming them?
> To long for things and regard them as [external] things –
> how does that compare to arranging things in patterns and never losing them?
> To yearn for whatever gives birth to things –
> how does that compare to possessing what brings them to completion? (*Xunzi* 17.10)

For Xunzi, then, rituals are not merely received practices, nor convenient social institutions; they are practicable forms in which the sages aimed to encapsulate the fundamental patterns of the universe. No human being, not even a sage, can know Heaven, but we can know Heaven's Way, which is the surest path to a flourishing and blessed life. Because human beings have limited knowledge and abilities, it is difficult for us to attain this deep understanding, and therefore the sages handed down the rituals to help us follow in their footsteps.

There is a radically different understanding of Xunzi than the one advanced here; Kurtis Hagen,[37] the most articulate exponent of this other view, contends that the Xunzi's Way is not an unchanging cosmological reality to which we must conform, but something constructed by human beings. There is one interesting passage that might be taken as support for Hagen's interpretation: "The Way is not the Way of Heaven (*tian zhi dao* 天之道), nor the Way of Earth (*di zhi dao* 帝之道); it is what people regard as the Way (*suo yi dao* 所以道), what the noble man is guided by (*suo dao* 所道)" (*Xunzi* 8.3). This seems to say, despite all the material in *Xunzi* 17 about apprehending the constancy of Heaven and then applying it profitably to daily life, that we are supposed to disregard the Way of Heaven, and create our own Way instead! Yang Liang 楊倞 (fl. 818 CE), the author of the oldest extant commentary to the *Xunzi*, evidently recognized this problem, and tried to soften the impact of *Xunzi* 8.3 by making it fit with the rest of the text: "This emphasizes that the Way of the Former Kings was not a matter of *yin* and *yang*, or mountains and rivers, or omens and prodigies, but the Way that people practice."

Yang Liang's opinion is surely not decisive; he was but an interpreter of Xunzi, not Xunzi himself, and his glosses are not always regarded as the most compelling today. But in this case I think he was right that Xunzi meant to say no more than that the Way is to be found not in prodigies and other freakish occurrences, but in the "constancies" that people can put into practice. Indeed, the very notion that the Way of Heaven, the Way of Earth, and the Way of human beings are distinct entities would contradict a point that Xunzi makes more than once: there is only one Way. "There are no two Ways in the world, and the Sage is never of two minds" (*Xunzi* 21.1). This single and holistic Way, moreover, serves as the enduring standard for all times because all ramified truths of the universe are unified within it:

It is said: There are those who have honed their skill at the Way, and those who have honed their skill at things. Those who have honed their skill at things treat each separate thing as a separate thing; those who have honed their skill at the Way treat each separate thing as part of an all-inclusive thing. Thus the noble man derives unity from the Way, and uses it as an aid in canvassing things. Since he derives unity from the Way, he is rectified; since he uses it as an aid in canvassing things, he is perspicacious; and since he advances perspicacious theories with a rectified will, he is the officer of all the myriad things. (*Xunzi* 21.6b)[38]

The Way is the correct scale for past and present; if one departs from the Way and chooses on the basis of one's own innards, then one does not know whence ruination and fortune are sent. (*Xunzi* 22.6b)

Therefore, what I think is meant by *tian zhi dao* and *di zhi dao* in *Xunzi* 8.3 is not "the Way of Heaven" and "the Way of Earth" – for that would wrongly imply that there are multiple discrete Ways – but "the Way *as it pertains to* Heaven" and "the Way *as it pertains* to Earth". (Classical Chinese permits this sort of syntactic flexibility.) What we need to understand is the Way as it pertains to human beings. Unusual celestial phenomena such as shooting stars must, theoretically, be explainable by a comprehensive formulation of the Way – there can be no *violations* of the Way in the natural world – but this is exactly why we do not aim for a comprehensive formulation of the Way. We can safely ignore shooting stars as irrelevant to human beings because they do not provide replicable patterns for use in moral and social development. Responding to the seasons with timely planting and harvesting is, once again, a more productive model.

This reading also coheres with Xunzi's distinctive theory of omens. Xunzi argued strongly against the old idea that weird occurrences on earth can be rationalized as monitory signs from Heaven.

When stars shoot down and trees squall, the citizens are all terrified. They say, "What is this?" I say, "It is nothing". These are the shifts in Heaven and Earth, transformations of *yin* and *yang*, material anomalies. It is acceptable to wonder at them, but it is not acceptable to fear them. No generation has been without eclipses of the sun and moon, untimely winds and rains, or the appearance of wondrous stars. If the ruler is enlightened and the government peaceful, then even if such things arise all together, they cannot cause any harm. If the ruler is benighted and the government precarious, then even if none of these things should happen, [their absence] will still confer no benefit.   (*Xunzi* 17.7)

What is crucial is not how loudly the trees may have squalled this year, but how people have behaved. Xunzi goes on to expound his theory of "human portents" (*renyao* 人祆), a term that would have seemed as outlandish in Xunzi's language as it does in ours. "Human portents" are the many shortsighted and immoral acts through which human beings bring on their own destruction.

Among material [anomalies] that may occur, it is human portents that are to be feared: poor ploughing that harms the harvest, hoeing and weeding out of season, governmental malice that causes the loss of the people. When agriculture is untimely and the harvest bad, the price of grain is high and the people starve. In the roads and streets there are dead people. These are called human portents. When governmental commands are unenlightened, corvée miscalculated or untimely, fundamental affairs chaotic – these are called human portents. When ritual and morality are not cultivated; when internal and external are not separated; when male and female are licentious and disorderly; when father and son are suspicious of each other; when superior and inferior are obstinate and estranged; when crime and hardship occur together – these are called human portents. Portents are born of disorder; when these three types [of human portents][39] obtain, there is no peace in the country.
                 (*Xunzi* 17.7)

Heaven has no part in such affairs. Now and then strange things may happen in the skies, but they have happened at all moments in history, and they have never been sufficient to destroy a prudent and moral society – whereas an imprudent and immoral society will fail even if it is spared an eclipse. Good acts have good consequences; bad acts have bad consequences; and only fools (and hypocrites) wait for Heaven to intercede.[40]

Xunzi even extends this theory of "human portents" to contend that religious ceremonies have no numinous effect; we carry them out merely for their inherent beauty and the social cohesion that they promote. In this connection, he has been compared to Durkheim.[41]

> If the sacrifice for rain [is performed], and it rains, what of it? I say: It is nothing. Even if there had been no sacrifice, it would have rained. When the sun and moon are eclipsed, we rescue them [i.e. by performing the proper rites]; when Heaven sends drought we perform the sacrifice for rain; we decide great matters only after divining with turtle and milfoil. This is not in order to obtain what we seek, but in order to embellish [such occasions]. Thus the noble man takes [these ceremonies] to be embellishment, but the populace takes them to be spiritual. To take them as embellishment is auspicious; to take them as spiritual is inauspicious.
>
> (*Xunzi* 17.8)

* * *

Xunzi's idea of manmade rituals based on immutable cosmic norms, which is distinctive among classical Confucians, can be used to test some of the questionable chapters in the *Xunzi*, such as the fifteenth chapter, entitled "Discussion of Warfare" ("Yibing" 議兵), which is presented as a debate between Xun Kuang and a certain Lord Linwu 臨武君 before King Xiaocheng of Zhao 趙孝成王 (r. 265–245 BCE).[42] The scholars of the Doubting-Antiquity School (*yigu pai* 疑古派 or *yigu xuechao* 疑古學潮)[43] of the 1920s and 1930s generally agreed that the "Discussion of Warfare" was written not by Xun Kuang but by his disciples, who silently inserted it into their teacher's collection for the benefit of later readers, because the chapter consistently refers to Xunzi as "Master Chamberlain Sun".[44] Not everyone was sure of the significance of this observation. Some scholars suggested that in writing about the philosophy of Xunzi, it is best to avoid the "Discussion of Warfare", along with the handful of other chapters that use the name "Master Chamberlain Sun", just to be safe. Others asserted that, from a philosophical point of view, there are no great contradictions between these chapters and the rest of the collection.

On the one hand, the name "Master Chamberlain Sun" does prove beyond doubt that the received version of the chapter cannot have been written by Xun Kuang himself. Moreover, the use of the posthumous name of King Xiaocheng of Zhao implies that the chapter was, at the very least, edited after 245 BCE (It is uncertain whether Xunzi himself was still alive at this time.)[45] And there is no reason why the date of the text could not be even later than that.[46]

It is also correct, however, that the "Discussion of Warfare" squares extremely well with Xunzi's undisputed writings – so well, in fact, that the author, whoever he was, must have been intimately familiar with Xunzi's philosophy, and applied it cogently to the question of warfare. Similarly, while it is uncertain whether the debate between Xun Kuang and Lord Linwu really took place – or, if it did, whether the chapter faithfully reproduces the participants' arguments – it is still possible that we are dealing with a very close approximation of what Xun Kuang once said in a live debate on warfare. To be sure, the figure of "Master Chamberlain Sun" assumes an oratorical tone in the "Discussion of Warfare" unlike that of his expository works, but a difference in register is only to be expected in material that was not originally composed in essay form.

The debate begins with some pronouncements by Lord Linwu, which are profoundly influenced by the famous military manual *Sunzi* 孫子. Lord Linwu discusses such considerations as surprise tactics and timely mobilizations: "Observe the enemy's movements; 'set out after him but arrive before him'. This is the essential technique in using troops" (*Xunzi* 15.1a). "Set out after him but arrive before him", as John Knoblock has pointed out, is an unmistakable quotation from the *Sunzi*.[47] Xunzi responds by denying the long-term value of clever battlefield manoeuvres. For the basis of all military action lies not in skilful generalship, but in "unifying the people".

By practising "humanity and morality", Xunzi argues, a sage ruler can undermine the power of an aggressor:

> Moreover, whom would the ruler of a cruel state send [to the battlefield]? Those whom he would send must be his own people. But his people would feel intimate toward us; they would be as complaisant as if we were their father and mother. They would be as attracted to us as to the pepper and orchid [i.e. sweet-smelling plants]. But when they look back at their ruler, then he will seem like a brand or a tattoo, like a sworn enemy. (*Xunzi* 15.1b)

In other words, even with brilliant strategies, a ruler cannot rely on his army if his people do not serve him gladly; and conversely, a benevolent ruler – one who deserves the name "King" – can always be sure of victory, because the soldiers of his enemy will simply desert their commander. Xunzi continues:

> Thus the troops of one who is a King are never tested. When Tang and Wu punished Jie and Zhòu 紂, they bowed with their hands folded and gave the signal with their finger, whereupon not one of the mighty and cruel states failed to rush to their service. (*Xunzi* 15.1d)

As he has related it so far, Xunzi's view of warfare is not original. The idea that a sage can evoke unquestioning devotion, even in his enemies, is commonplace in Confucian discussions of warfare. Mencius, for example, also argued that a beneficent ruler will always defeat his opponents in battle, because in winning over the people, he secures for himself the most effective weapon of all. Even the *Sunzi* agrees that the most skilled general will subdue his enemy's troops without having to fight them.[48] (Perhaps Lord Linwu has forgotten this point; the tactics that he emphasizes are to be used, according to the *Sunzi*, only when battle is inevitable.)

What is unique in Xunzi's "Discussion of Warfare", however, is his emphasis on ritual as the key to a well-ordered state. To be sure, earlier writings had also discussed the idea of ritual as the foundation of statecraft, and the *Zuo Commentary to the Springs and Autumns* (*Zuozhuan* 左傳), in particular, is famous for its scenes in which a ruler who is about to attack his neighbour publicly justifies his aggression on the grounds that he is merely "punishing" his enemy's intolerable violations of ritual. But Xunzi raises the significance of ritual to a new level: in his view, the ruler's ability to govern his state in accordance with ritual is the sole criterion that will determine success or failure on the battlefield.

> If the ruler is talented, his state will be ordered; if the ruler is incompetent, the state will be chaotic. If he exalts ritual and esteems morality, his state will be ordered; if he is lax about rituals and discountenances morality, his state will be disordered. (*Xunzi* 15.1c)

Having established the principle that "exalting ritual" is the true path to order and strength, Xunzi proceeds to expatiate on the concept of ritual in characteristic language.

> Ritual is the ridgepole of order and discrimination; it is the foundation of a strong state, the Way of awesome practice, the chief precondition for a successful reputation. When kings and dukes follow [the rituals], that is how they obtain the world; when they do not follow them, that is how they bring about the perdition of their altars of soil and grain. Thus firm armour and keen weapons are not enough to bring about victory; lofty fortifications and deep moats are not enough to bring about security; strict commands and manifold punishments are not enough to instil awe. If one follows the Way, then one will progress; if one does not follow the Way, then one will perish. (*Xunzi* 15.4)

One will notice that the rituals are repeatedly associated with the Way in these passages; at times, the two terms appear to be used interchangeably, as though "exalting the rituals" were essentially the same thing as "following the Way". The figure of Master Chamberlain Xun in the "Discussion of Warfare" evidently views military combat as one of the many fields of analysis that can be engaged profitably with the fundamental and all-encompassing model of the Way manifested through ritual practice.[49] The chapter is not really about warfare at all.

* * *

So too Xunzi's famous essay on language, "Rectifying Names" ("Zhengming" 正名): while it includes some impressive insights into the nature of verbal communication,[50] the primary concern of the chapter is morality, not linguistics. Modern readers have sometimes missed the thrust of the essay because a few of Xunzi's comments sound as though they came out of a twentieth-century pragmatics textbook:[51]

> Names have no inherent appropriateness. We designate them [by some word] in order to name them. If it is fixed by convention and implemented by custom, then it is called appropriate. If [the name that people use] is different from what has been agreed upon, then it is called inappropriate.
>
> (*Xunzi* 22.2g)

Does this not sound exactly like Saussure?[52]

But Xunzi was not interested in the same questions as modern linguists. In "Rectifying Names", Xunzi also discusses sophistic paradoxes that were rampant in his day (the most famous being "A white horse is not a horse"),[53] dividing them into three typological categories. His conclusion discloses that his main purpose is not a proper taxonomy of falsidical paradoxes,[54] but an assertion of the moral purpose of language: "All heretical theories and aberrant sayings depart from the correct Way and are presumptuously crafted according to these three categories of delusion" (*Xunzi* 22.3d). The paradoxes of the sophists cannot be used as a basis for moral governance, and thus would be objectionable even if they were not in fact false; they are "disputes with no use" (*Xunzi* 6.6). The only legitimate purpose of language, like that of government itself, is to serve as the king's tool in propagating moral excellence.

> When one who is a king determines names, if names are fixed and realities distinguished, if the Way is practised and his intentions communicated, then he may cautiously lead the people and unify them by this means. Thus splitting phrases and presumptuously creating [new] names in order to bring disorder on rectified names causes the people to be doubtful and confused. When there are many disputes and indictments among people, this is called "great sedition"; this crime is as [serious as] crimes pertaining to [the falsification of] contracts and measures. ... When one's people dare not circulate odd phrases to bring disorder on rectified names, they will be unified by the Way and its methods, and will be careful to obey [the king's] orders. In such a case, his traces will be long-lasting. To have long-lasting traces and to achieve merit is the acme of establishing order. This is what is achieved by carefully defending the convention of names. (*Xunzi* 22.1c)

Note that the task of determining names and then enforcing their use belongs to the king alone, not to any lord and certainly not to the people. "One who is a king" (*wangzhe* 王者), in Confucian language, refers not to the person who happens to be sitting on the throne, but someone who has lived up to the moral requirements of that office and duly rules the world by his charismatic example. Accordingly, phrases like "leading and unifying the people" refer not to expedient rulership, but to implementing the Confucian project of morally transforming the world. Language is useful in that enterprise because without it the people cannot even understand the ruler's wishes, let alone carry them out.

Just as the rituals need to be based on the foundation of the Way, the ruler's names, though they can be arbitrary as designations, must correspond to reality. You can make up the word for "reality", but you cannot make up reality.

What does one rely upon to [determine] same and different?
I say: One relies upon the senses. The senses of all members
of the same species with the same essence – their senses perceive things in the same manner. Thus we associate things
that appear similar upon comparison; in this manner we
provide designated names for them in order to define them
with respect to each other. Shape, body, colour and pattern
are distinguished by the eyes. Sound, tone, treble, bass, mode,
harmony – diverse sounds are distinguished by the ears.
Sweet, bitter, salty, bland, pungent, sour – diverse tastes are
distinguished by the mouth. Fragrant, foul, sweet-smelling,
odorous, rank, fetid, putrid, acrid – diverse smells are distinguished by the nose. Painful, itchy, cold, hot, smooth,
sharp, light and heavy are differentiated by the body. Statements, reasons, happiness, resentment, grief, joy, love, hate
and desire are distinguished by the heart-mind.

(Xunzi 22.2c–d)

The notion that we rely upon our senses to perceive the world around
us represents a substantial claim on Xunzi's part, because other philosophers, such as Zhuangzi, had already suggested that reality is
not straightforwardly discerned; on the contrary, one's partial perspective on reality necessarily informs one's perception of it. This
was, essentially, Zhuangzi's argument in "Discourse on the Equal-
ity of Things" ("Qiwu lun" 齊物論).[55] For Xunzi, however, reality is
reality, regardless of how we perceive it. Once again, scholars like
Hagen[56] question whether Xunzi is such a strong realist, but I find
any alternative, "constructivist" interpretation of Xunzi difficult to
reconcile with his repeated assertions that language must conform
to reality and the Way.

Names are that by which one defines different real objects
(*shi* 實).[57] Phrases are that by which one combines the names
of different real objects in order to expound a single idea.
Polemical statements are that by which one analogizes about
the movements of the Way without causing names to diverge

from reality. Definitions and names are what polemical persuasions use [as their basis]. Polemical statements are what the heart-mind uses to depict the Way. The heart-mind is the master craftsman of the Way. The Way is the canonical pattern of order. One's heart-mind should accord with the Way, one's statements with one's heart-mind, one's phrases with one's statements. (*Xunzi* 22.3f)

With the heart-mind, we come at last to the keystone of Xunzi's philosophy, the one piece that links together all the others. The Chinese word, *xin* 心, meaning "heart", is the same that Mencius had used, but Xunzi attributes such strong and varied mental processes to this organ that one has to construe it as not only the heart but also the mind.

First, the heart-mind is the organ that we use to discover the Way. Xunzi's discussion of Heaven presented his argument that moral self-cultivation is a matter of correctly perceiving and then applying the Way, but it did not explain how we perceive the Way in the first place. Elsewhere, he addresses the question explicitly:

How does one know the Way? I say: the heart-mind. How does the heart-mind know? I say: emptiness, unity and tranquillity. The heart-mind never stops storing, but it has something called "emptiness". The heart-mind never stops being filled, but it has something called "unity". The heart-mind never stops moving, but it has something called "tranquillity". From birth humans have awareness; with awareness come thoughts; thoughts are stored. But [the heart-mind] has something called "emptiness": it does not take what is stored to harm what is to be received; this is called "emptiness". From birth the heart-mind has awareness; with awareness comes differentiation; different things are known at the same time. Knowing different things at the same time is duality. But [the heart-mind] has something called "unity": it does not take one thing to harm another; this is called "unity". The heart-mind dreams when it sleeps; it moves spontaneously when it relaxes; it plans when it is employed. Thus the

> heart-mind never stops moving, but it has something called "tranquillity": it does not take dreams and fancies to bring disorder upon knowledge; this is called "tranquillity".
>
> (*Xunzi* 21.5d)

What Xunzi called "emptiness", "unity" and "tranquillity" – terms self-consciously borrowed from the Daoist tradition[58] – are three nurturable faculties that we all possess from birth, but do not all employ to the same degree. (The title of Chapter 21, "Resolving Blindness", refers to the self-destructive acts that people undertake because they fail to employ their heart-minds correctly.) "Emptiness" refers to the heart-mind's ability to store a seemingly unlimited amount of information; we do not have to erase one datum in order to make room for another. "Unity" refers to the heart-mind's ability to synthesize diverse data into meaningful paradigms. And "tranquillity" refers to the heart-mind's ability to distinguish fantasy from rational thinking. Armed with these powers, we can infer the patterns of the Way by taking in, and then pondering, the data transmitted to the heart-mind by the senses.

Second, the heart-mind is the chief among the organs. It is the only organ that can command the others; indeed, it is the only organ with any self-consciousness.

> The mind is the lord of the body and the master of "godlike insight" (*shenming* 神明).[59] It issues commands but does not receive commands. It prohibits on its own; it employs on its own; it considers on its own; it takes on its own; it acts on its own; it ceases on its own. Thus the mouth can be forced to be silent or to speak; the body can be forced to contract or expand; the mind cannot be forced to change its intention. If it accepts [something], it receives it; if it rejects, it forgoes it.
>
> (*Xunzi* 21.6a)

Third, because the heart-mind can control both itself and all other organs of the body, it is the font of "artifice", or the deliberate actions that begin to transform the morally deficient *xing*:

When the heart-mind reasons and the other faculties put it into action – this is called "artifice". When reasoning is accumulated in this manner and the other faculties practise it, so that [morality] is brought to completion – this is called "artifice".   (*Xunzi* 22.1b)

And most explicitly:

People's desire for life is deep; their hatred of death is deep. Yet when people discard life and cause their own death, this is not because they do not desire life or because they desire death. Rather, this is because it is not possible for them to live; it is possible for them only to die. Thus when one's desires are excessive but one's actions do not reach [the same degree], it is because the heart-mind brings them to a halt. If the heart-mind has accepted correct patterns, then even if one's desires are manifold, how would they harm order? And when one's desires do not reach [the level of excess], but one's actions are excessive, it is because the heart-mind causes one [to act in this manner]. If the mind has accepted invalid patterns, then even if one's desires are few, how would one refrain from disorder? Thus order and disorder lie with whatever the heart-mind will accept, and not with the desires or the emotions.

                                                                 (*Xunzi* 22.5a)

The human instinct of self-preservation must be the starkest example of *xing*, yet the heart-mind is capable of overriding even this impulse by "halting" it if it clashes with the "correct patterns". We have the necessary faculties to recognize immorality when we see it, and if we permit ourselves to tread an immoral path, we cannot blame our emotions or desires, but must accept that our heart-mind has failed to exert the requisite discipline. We know that we could have done better. Indeed, when we speak of "we", we are speaking of our heart-mind.[60] For the heart-mind is the crucible where these teeming moral deliberations take place.

Thus Xunzi ends, like all Confucians, with individual responsibility. Mencius would have called this "living up to our destiny"; for Xunzi, with his vastly more ramified cosmology, it is more accurately stated as the heart-mind's obligation to process the principles of the Way and then command the rest of the body to conform. Because we are not sages, we are advised to follow the rituals in order to attain this degree of understanding, but, fundamentally, the path to morality is open to anyone who sees and thinks.

FIVE

Neo-Confucianism and Confucianism today

The task of this final chapter is to outline the course of post-classical Confucianism, concluding with a consideration of the status of Confucianism in the Chinese world today.

Xunzi lived long enough to observe the emergence of the state of Qin – the likeliest source of the name "China"[1] – and may even have seen the establishment of the empire under the First Emperor of Qin in 221 BCE. The Qin dynasty (221–207 BCE), and the longer-lived Han dynasty that soon succeeded it, were not initially beholden to Confucianism. Although it is true that the Qin government funded academicians (*boshi* 博士) specializing in each of the canonical Confucian texts,[2] its law code, as we can discern from legal manuscripts recovered from a tomb at Shuihudi 睡虎地, was not based on Confucian principles.[3] Rather, the main purpose of the Qin laws seems to have been to spell out the various categories of subjects' obligations to the state, as well as the penalties for failing to live up to them (which depended on rank and legal status).

The earliest known Han-dynasty legal texts (recently discovered in a tomb at Zhangjiashan 張家山) display wholesale borrowing from Qin precedents, even repeating statutes verbatim. The attitude of the state was, as before, that family matters such as household disputes should not normally come before its courts;[4] rather, cases that warranted state intervention were those in which some defendant (or party of defendants) could be held responsible for failing to discharge specified duties. Confucian scholars had no special influence in these early decades of the Han, and could be subjected to humiliation by the imperial house – as in the case of Master Yuan Gu 轅固生, a scholar who was ordered to fight a boar because his Confucian-oriented harangues had begun to grate on Empress Dowager Dou 竇太后 (205–135 BCE), who adored the *Laozi*.[5]

Over time, however, the Han state found it convenient to portray itself as a benevolent government in contrast to the notorious excesses of the Qin, and Confucian ideology proved to be among the handiest tools in this legitimation effort. The resulting shift in orientation is especially clear in the legal sphere. In contrast to the narrower conception of the swath of law in the Shuihudi and Zhangjiashan texts, private and familial relations were now accepted as areas subject to regulation by the state, which also adopted Confucian principles in adjudicating such cases. For example, vengeance killings motivated by filial piety, for which defendants would previously have been sentenced as murderers without further ado, were now the subject of considerable jurisprudential agony, inasmuch as the state felt compelled to recognize the legitimacy of filial piety as a motive even for serious crimes.[6] The noted historian Ban Gu 班固 (32–92 CE), for his part, held that laws were counterproductive in so far as they failed to advance Confucian moral principles, and argued for scrapping the current legal code in favour of a new and simpler corpus based on the Confucian canon.[7]

But the Han dynasty eventually collapsed, and in the period of intellectual re-evaluation that followed, Xunzi's standing fell as his philosophy came to be identified, rightly or wrongly, as the ideological foundation of the failed imperial state, which was reviled by many as propagating artificial ritualism, counterfeit erudition, and an oppressive network of laws that serve only to interfere with the innocuous enjoyment of life.[8] In the ensuing era of political division, known as the Northern and Southern dynasties (317–589 CE), literati turned in increasing numbers to other religious traditions, such as Daoism and Buddhism. As late as the Tang dynasty (618–906), Han Yu decried China's rejection of Confucianism, but also recognized that he was out of step with the rest of the literati, who still regarded Confucianism as but one of the three legitimate traditions. Tang emperors regarded themselves as patrons of Daoism and Buddhism no less than of Confucianism, and Han's outspoken criticism of the emperor's veneration of a supposed relic of the Buddha nearly cost him his life.[9]

It was not until the Confucian revival in the Song dynasty (960–1279) that Han Yu was acclaimed as a genius whose society was not ready for him. Neo-Confucianism, a vague term that Western scholars have adopted to refer to various strands of Confucian thinking in this period,[10] merits more extended comments here. Prominent early Neo-Confucians, such as Ouyang Xiu 歐陽修 (1007–72), did not intend a thorough reinterpretation of Confucianism so much as a more comprehensive application of it in politics. Ouyang believed that gentlemen talented and fortunate enough to qualify for high office had a moral responsibility to use their national influence to good ends. One characteristic statement of his beliefs is "A Discourse on the Partisanship of Friends" ("Pengdang lun" 朋黨論),[11] where he argues that partisanship is not inherently objectionable; what matters are the goals to which a political faction commits itself. If that faction pursues the correct moral principles, it can do a world of good. At the same time, Ouyang was an impeccable stylist who believed that flawless expression was as important (and rare) as thoughtful reading and reflection.[12]

Other Neo-Confucians, however, not only wished to see more Confucian projects among the scholar-officialdom, but also offered a radically new cosmological framework for traditional Confucian ideas. Cheng Yi 程頤 (1033–1107), for example, one of the founders of *daoxue* 道學 philosophy,[13] provided a theoretical justification for reading the classics that accorded with his novel metaphysical postulates. All matter, according to Cheng Yi and his elder brother, Cheng Hao 程顥 (1032–85), was made up of two components, *li* 理 and *qi* 氣.[14] *Qi* is the easier of the two to translate; as in Mencius, it still means "matter". For *li*, on the other hand, scholars have proposed renderings as varied as "pattern", "principle" and "coherence".[15] *Qi* denotes the physical substance of an object, *li* its form and underlying structure. *Daoxue* philosophers were strict naturalists in that *li* is both the "reason why [something] is the way it is" and the "rule by which it ought to be".[16] The Chengs maintained further that there is only one fundamental *li* of the cosmos; differences appear only in the many manifestations of *li*.

The duty of the noble man is to try to apprehend that *li* and live by it. This is called *gewu*: "to arrive at [hence: to investigate] things" (taken from *Great Learning*). And since *li* is immanent in all things, *gewu* can be achieved by different methods: the study of books, and explanation of the moral principles in them; discussion of prominent figures, past and present, in order to distinguish what is right and wrong in their actions; and even practical experience.[17] By reading books and apprehending the *li* inherent in them, Cheng Yi says, one can learn about the world. Once *li* is discovered, the student can "extend the *li*" (*tuili* 推理), or analogize, and gain insight into the workings of the cosmos.

> In investigating things to exhaust their principles, the idea is not that one must exhaust completely everything in the world. If they are exhausted in only one matter, for the rest one can infer by analogy. Taking filial piety as an example, what is the reason why behavior is considered filial? If you cannot exhaust the principles in one matter, do so in another, whether you deal with an easy or a difficult example first depending on the depth of your knowledge. Just so there are innumerable paths by which you can get to the capital, and it is enough to find one of them. The reason why they can be exhausted is simply that there is one principle in all the innumerable things, and even a single thing or activity, however small, has this principle.[18]

Not all books, however, are equally suited to this sort of enterprise, as Zhu Xi (1130–1200), whose line of teachers went back directly to Cheng Yi, emphasized. The classics embody *li* because they were written by the sages, who knew the *li* of the universe. Other books, by unenlightened authors, convey no such cosmic principle; and even the classics themselves, if read by unprepared students, can be misleading. Thus Zhu Xi insisted that reading the classics constituted one of the most efficient ways of getting at *li*, and cautioned that one must read only the right books in order to benefit from them. Zhu was critical, for example, of his friend Lü Zuqian 呂祖謙 (1137–81), who devoted great amounts of time to the study of history.[19] Cheng Yi himself had said that the study of "prominent figures, past and present", could serve as one way of *gewu*, but Zhu warned that Lü was wasting his time with trivia. *Li* was right there in the classics, for all to read.

Zhu Xi consciously developed his theory of reading (*dushufa* 讀書法: "the method of reading books") along lines laid down by the Cheng brothers: "Today's scholars have never understood the main point of learning. One should simply probe moral principle."[20] And one of the best ways of probing moral principle is reading:

> The words of the sages and worthies for the most part seem dissimilar. Yet they've always been interconnected. For example, the Master said, "Do not look, listen, speak, or move, unless it be in accordance with the rites" [an abbreviation of *Analects* 12.1]; "when abroad, behave as though you were receiving an important guest, and when employing the services of the common people, behave as though you were officiating at an important sacrifice" [*Analects* 12.2]; and "be loyal and true in your every word, serious and mentally attentive in all that you do" [*Analects* 15.6]. Mencius then said, "Seek for the lost mind" [*Mencius* 6A.11], and "preserve the mind and nourish the nature" [*Mencius* 7A.1]. ... [Zhu continues with more examples.] If you simply read all this, it may seem like a hodge-podge, utterly confused. But in fact it's all of the same principle.[21]

The several passages that Zhu quotes might seem "like a hodge-podge", and scholars before and after Zhu Xi have pointed out many instances in which the classics do not appear to agree (concerning questions of both fact and opinion). But "the interrelatedness of the classical texts", as one scholar has observed, "was an article of faith for Zhu Xi".[22] They are all united by *li*. If you are confused, you simply have not understood. As Zhu Xi conceded, to become so conversant with the texts that one can discern the principle within them, one must dedicate most of one's time to pursuing a rigorous classical curriculum. Zhu Xi's form of *daoxue* was a lifelong calling.

Zhu Xi was one of the most influential philosophers in all of Chinese history, and his deep-seated belief in the virtues of classical learning attracted many intellectuals after his death. But later generations began to question the supposition that one had to devote oneself to Zhu's kind of reading in order to reach philosophical maturity. Indeed, even some of Zhu's contemporaries were suspicious of the dominant place of reading in his programme. Lu Jiuyuan 陸九淵 (1139–93), Zhu's chief rival, is famous for having said, "If, in studying, we know the root, then all the Six Canons are our footnotes".[23] Lu was taking a familiar point of view: *li* does not reside only in books.[24]

A watershed in the history of Neo-Confucianism and in the attitude toward book learning and the study of the past appears in the work of the eremite Liu Yin 劉因 (1249–93). Liu revered Zhu Xi as a sage who, like Confucius and the other ancient culture heroes, had attained a thorough understanding of *li* and had embodied the Way in his life. But Liu could not ignore Zhu's own injunction that one must "obtain it by oneself" (*zide* 自得).[25] As Tu Wei-ming writes:

> Despite Liu's whole-hearted devotion to Zhu Xi and, for that matter, Song Learning in general, he was committed to the idea of an independent mind as the ultimate judge of relevance and value. He ... insisted that one's 'innate knowledge' (*liangzhi* 良知) must not be swayed by opinions from outside, even if they are as authoritative as the teachings of the Song masters."[26]

"Innate knowledge" is an allusion to one of the most important of the ancient classics, *Mencius* 7A.15, where *liangzhi* is defined as "what one knows without thinking" (*suo bu lü er zhi zhe* 所不慮而知者).

Liu is making a solid Mencian argument: we are endowed with the potential for wisdom, and must return to our innate intelligence to determine right and wrong before we let ourselves be coloured by external influences. In this manner, Liu Yin, a philosopher who was convinced of Zhu Xi's authority, explained, in perfect conformity with the classics, why he could not learn anything from Zhu's writings directly.

For the next several centuries, the place of book learning was the subject of continuing dispute. Figures like Chen Xianzhang 陳獻章 (1428–1500) worried that reading might become a kind of game for well-intentioned, but unfocused, scholars:

> In the study of books, never be tied down to the text.
> A thousand and ten thousand volumes are but dregs.[27]

Critics of a more conservative bent, however, charged that students who neglected the classics were hurling themselves headlong into meditative Buddhism – anathema to sober Confucians. The debate raged on as one of the most critical forces shaping contemporary intellectual life. Most literati felt compelled to voice an opinion on the question of the merits of book learning.

But wherever one stood in this matter, there was never any question that the debate was consequential. Both camps insisted that their view was authoritative *on textual grounds*. The issue was one of exegesis, and all the participants in the debate agreed that the classics themselves held the answer; what differed were particular interpretations. By the end of the Chinese Empire in 1912, however, the classics were becoming desanctified, as the fledgling nation began to ask itself whether its classical heritage was still relevant. The alliance between classical scholarship and the imperial agenda, which had for centuries allowed scholastic study to flourish, undermined the credibility of classicism in the minds of early twentieth-century intellectuals. The marriage rankled moderns who perceived that for centuries, dynasty and orthodoxy had subsisted in symbiosis. After China's last imperial house had come crashing to the ground, observers in both China and the West embarked upon a thorough re-evaluation of China's classical legacy, and scrutinized the classic texts as part of a past that had failed.

A good example of this revisionist sentiment in Europe can be found in the writings of Max Weber (1864–1920). "[Chinese] education", Weber remarked, "was transmitted only through the study of the old classics whose absolutely canonical prestige and purified form of orthodoxy went without question. ... The whole of Confucianism became a relentless canonization of tradition."[28] It is an oft-repeated criticism: Confucianism impedes creativity and progress by glorifying those who have come before us and those who are placed in a position of authority over us. Talcott Parsons later echoed Weber:

> [Traditionalism] is so powerful that it requires forces of exceptional strength to break through it even appreciably, and only when that has happened are certain kinds of social development, like that of rational bourgeois capitalism, possible. Not only did the Confucian ethic ... fail to do this; on the contrary it provided a direct and powerful sanction of the traditional order.[29]

Parsons referred to Weber's most famous indictment of Confucianism: it prevented the development of capitalism in China. Having already published his *Protestant Ethic and the Spirit of Capitalism*, Weber undertook in 1920–21 a thorough study of Chinese religion and society as part of a grand empirical investigation of his thesis that the Protestant ethic contributed to the rise of capitalism in the West. Weber saw a fundamental distinction in the way that Puritans and Confucians have observed the world and their own place in it:

> The typical Confucian used his own and his family's savings in order to acquire a literary education and to have himself trained for the examinations. Thus he gained the basis for a cultured status position. The typical Puritan earned plenty, spent little, and reinvested his income as capital in rational capitalist enterprise out of an asceticist compulsion to save. ... Only the Puritan rational ethic with its supra-mundane

orientation brought economic rationalism to its consistent conclusion. This happened merely because nothing was further from the conscious Puritan intention. It happened because inner-worldly work was simply expressive of the striving for a transcendental goal. The world, as promised, fell to Puritanism because the Puritans alone "had striven for God and his justice". … Nothing conflicted more with the Confucian ideal of gentility than the idea of a "vocation". The "princely" man was an aesthetic value; he was not a tool of a god. But the true Christian, the other-worldly and inner-worldly asceticist, wished to be nothing more than a tool of his God; in this he sought his dignity. Since this is what he wished to be, he was a useful instrument for rationally transforming and mastering the world.[30]

Confucians, in other words, attempted to adjust themselves to the world rather than to master it; Protestants, wishing to be the instruments of their Lord, transformed the world by accumulating wealth.

That the Confucian gentleman abhorred the idea of being a tool or a professional is undeniable: "The noble man does not serve as a utensil", as Confucius declared (*Analects* 2.12). But recent critics have challenged Weber's claim by showing that Confucianism, far from being an obstacle, has played a decisive role in the economic revitalization of the East Asian states and city-states known as the "Four Little Dragons": South Korea, Taiwan, Hong Kong and Singapore. Ezra F. Vogel, for example, points to three specific attributes of Confucianism that have spurred the process of industrialization in East Asia: a meritocratic elite, a system of entrance examinations, and, above all, a sense of the importance of the group.[31] Scholarly opinion today tends to hold that the "failure" of Chinese capitalism, if it is even judicious to speak in such terms, is attributable to factors beyond the dominance of the Confucian ethic; and, in any case, if Confucianism has had an effect on the economy of East Asia, it has not always been negative.

While we may judge Weber's thesis to be historiographically insufficient, we must take care not to read it as merely the self-congratulatory pronouncement of a more fortunate foreigner. For Weber's opinions were paralleled on the other side of the globe by those of his Chinese contemporaries. In January of 1919, Chen Duxiu 陳獨秀 (1879–1942), Dean of Humanities at Peking University and an eventual co-founder of the Chinese Communist Party,[32] wrote in an article in his magazine, *New Youth* 新青年:

> They accused this magazine on the grounds that it intended to destroy Confucianism, the code of rituals, the "national quintessence", chastity of women, traditional ethics (loyalty, filial piety, chastity), traditional arts (the Chinese opera), traditional religion (ghosts and gods), and ancient literature, as well as old-fashioned politics (privileges and government by men alone).
>
> All of these charges are conceded. But we plead not guilty. We have committed the alleged crimes only because we supported the two gentlemen, Mr. Democracy and Mr. Science. In order to advocate Mr. Democracy, we are obliged to oppose Confucianism, the codes of rituals, chastity of women, traditional ethics, and old-fashioned politics; in order to advocate Mr. Science, we have to oppose traditional arts and traditional religion; and in order to advocate both Mr. Democracy and Mr. Science, we are compelled to oppose the cult of the "national quintessence" and ancient literature.[33]

Chen faulted Confucianism because he saw it as inimical not to capitalism – of which he was never enamoured – but to democracy and science. But the anti-Confucianism of the early Republic provoked responses almost immediately. Liang Qichao remarked that the West, fresh from the experience of the First World War, was growing weary of "Mr Science", even as Chinese radicals like Chen Duxiu were embracing him:

> Those who praised the omnipotence of science had hoped previously that, as soon as science succeeded, the golden age

would appear forthwith. Now science is successful indeed; material progress in the West in the last one hundred years has greatly surpassed the achievements of the three thousand years prior to this period. Yet we human beings have not secured happiness; on the contrary, science gives us catastrophes. We are like travelers losing their way in a desert. They see a big black shadow ahead, and desperately run to it, thinking that it may lead them somewhere. But after running a long way, they no longer see the shadow and fall into the slough of despond. What is that shadow? It is this "Mr. Science". The Europeans have dreamed a vast dream of the omnipotence of science; now they decry its bankruptcy. This is a major turning-point in current world thought.[34]

The promises of scientific Utopianism, Liang urged, are but a mirage. And while Liang Qichao was demonstrating the folly of accepting wholeheartedly the tarnished rationalist ideals in which the Europeans themselves were beginning to lose faith, other intellectuals argued that, despite their defects, the Chinese classics offer unique possibilities unmatched by other traditions. Liang Shuming 梁漱溟 (1893–1988) published a book to this effect in 1922: *Eastern and Western Cultures and Their Philosophies* (*Dong-Xi wenhua jiqi zhexue* 東西文化及其哲學). The two distinguishing characteristics of Western culture, Liang agreed, are indeed science and democracy, as Chen Duxiu had suggested; but the genius of Chinese civilization is intuitionism. Liang (manifestly influenced by Rabindranath Tagore)[35] attributed the differing fortunes of China and the West to the basic organizing principles of their philosophy: Western thought attempts to solve man's primal material needs, whereas Chinese thought addresses the concerns of the spirit.[36] Consequently, the West may have removed the basic problems of survival, but finds itself spiritually wanting; and although China is poor because its philosophy never sought to harness the forces of nature, the world must prepare for the coming Sinification and *Confucianization* of mankind.

All our points of inferiority are due to the disorderliness of our cultural evolution; [our culture] matured prematurely. {It is not that our attitude was wrong; it is that we were wrong in taking hold of this attitude too soon. This is the one reason why we have erred.} We did not continue to struggle with the forces of nature and conquer nature; as a consequence, we are now, in every way, thralls to nature. We did not wait to develop a concept of ego, but just passed over [that stage] and {went on to the concept of non-ego; we did not wait for the unfolding of individualism, but} put value on compromising the self and yielding to others, so now we are enslaved by myriad kinds of authority. We did not wait for the development of the intellect, but skipped [that stage] and went on to esteem illogical spirit and favor the use of intuition alone, so now our thought is muddled and our scholarship is unsystematic.[37]

However:

The attitude I want to put forth is the "resoluteness" of Confucius. ... Only this sort of dynamism can make up for the former Chinese shortcomings, save the Chinese from their present afflictions, avoid the faults of the Westerners, and enable the Chinese to cope with the needs of the world.[38]

Generalizations sometimes got the better of Liang Shuming, but his message resounded. For Liang's pro-Chinese and pro-Confucian spirit is continually apparent in twentieth-century discussions of the Chinese classics. On New Year's Day, 1958 – over three decades after the original publication of Liang's book – four of the most eminent scholars of Chinese thought, Zhang Junmai 張君勱 (i.e. Carsun Chang), Xu Fuguan 徐復觀, Tang Junyi 唐君毅 and Mou Zongsan 牟宗三, issued a joint statement entitled "A Manifesto for a Re-appraisal of Sinology and Reconstruction of Chinese Culture". The tenor is familiar: there is much that the West can learn from China. As Chang wrote in his English version of the Manifesto:

> In the first place, the West needs the spirit and capacity of sensing the presence of what *is* at every particular moment, and of giving up everything that can be had. The strength of the West's cultural spirit lies in its ability to push ahead indefinitely. However, there is no secure foundation underlying the feverish pursuit of progress. Along with this pursuit of progress there is a feeling of discontentment and of emptiness. In order to fill this emptiness, the individual and the nation constantly find new ways for progress and expansion. At the same time external obstructions and an internal exhaustion of energy cause the collapse of the individual and the nation. This is why the most powerful ancient Western nations collapsed and never did recover from their downfall. Chinese culture ... achieves the capacity to "accept what is self-sufficient at the moment". Chinese thought has always regarded "retreat" as more fundamental than "advance". Complementing the characteristically Western push for progress, this will provide a solid and secure foundation for Western civilization.[39]

It is clear from the defensive tone of the Manifesto that the problem of the Chinese past still engages the most sophisticated minds of East Asia. Parliaments and ministers debate to this day the extent to which their nations ought to preserve their Confucian heritage: how much Confucianism does one want in schools? Or in politics? Within the Communist Party, the discussions can be even more vexed. Was Confucianism good or bad for Chinese history? How should the government deal with Confucian studies today? Can Confucianism be gainfully dissociated from the allegedly "feudal" and "contradictory" society replaced by post-Marxist–Leninist–Mao Zedong–Deng Xiaoping Thought?[40]

The government of the People's Republic of China has recently taken a position almost diametrically opposed to the uncompromising denigration of Confucianism during the days of the "Criticize Lin [Biao] and Confucius" 批林批孔 campaign (1973–74). In the years after Mao's death, the central government experimented with subtle signals that it repudiated the Cultural Revolution without opening the door to unbridled censure, and by the late 1980s Confucius had emerged as the most readily inflatable icon for this purpose. New Confucians and likeminded traditionalists, taking heed of conspicuous government support for Confucian projects (such as lavishly funded "Confucius Institutes" in foreign universities), have offered some shrill endorsements. For example, Zhang Yimou's film *Wode fuqin muqin* 我的父親母親 (released in English as *The Road Home*, 1999) disparages the moral decay of the modern culture of convenience, and urges a return to tried-and-true Confucian norms. In view of Zhang's earlier and more satirical work, this is a startling message.

Paternalistic governments throughout China's history have been attracted to Confucius because they have regarded inculcating deference among the populace as a Confucian ideal. Were Confucius himself to have discovered how his teachings would be appropriated, he might not have been pleased. Confucian ethics begin with the premise that human beings have the capacity for moral self-cultivation, and thus a responsibility to reflect daily on their conduct and to modify it where it is deficient. Moreover, although Confucianism certainly does emphasize service to the state – as long as rulers make a serious effort to live up to the obligation of providing their subjects with an environment of moral excellence – it never approves of craven obedience. On the contrary, the highest form of Confucian loyalty is principled counsel and remonstrance. The duty of a Confucian adviser is to help his lord along the right moral path, and to dissuade him, in harsh terms if necessary, from pursuing immoral or self-defeating policies. Some rulers in Chinese history have valued remonstrance; others have not.

Thus it remains to be seen how long the present government's energetic patronage of Confucius will last. No amount of state sponsorship will make an idea stick if people are not truly convinced by it.[41] Confucius himself never bothered with students who did not thirst for his instruction. Most Chinese people today thirst for other things.

Manhood in the *Analects*

Is Confucianism sexist? Studies of Confucianism and gender tend to fixate on this question. Confucius's few and cryptic remarks about women have been thoroughly analysed and deconstructed, but little in the way of consensus has emerged, the material being simply too fragmentary. Extending the enquiry beyond the *Analects* to such texts as the *Odes*, *Discourses of the States* (*Guoyu* 國語), and *Zuo Commentary* yields a larger quantity of material from which to reconstruct classical Confucian gender discourse, but not everyone is inclined to accept these other materials as strictly Confucian – or, if they *are* Confucian, it is possible that they represent only a limited cross-section of the tradition. Thus the first problem with the question "Is Confucianism sexist?" is that we do not have sufficient documentation to provide a definitive answer.

Chenyang Li is one of the few participants in this debate to have approached the question from the other direction, that is, by considering not what Confucius had to say about women, but what he said about *men*. The result was his thesis that early Confucianism advanced a conception of ethics that is compatible with, and reminiscent of, contemporary feminism.[1] Li has both his supporters and his critics,[2] but one implication of his work seems undeniable: while so much has been written about the Confucian conception of womanhood, a serious study of Confucianism and gender must take into account Confucius's conception of *manhood*.[3]

Many of the relevant passages describe the so-called "noble man" (*junzi*). It seems appropriate to focus on the noble man, inasmuch as he is universally understood as male. I have never come across an ancient text in which a woman is described as a noble man (*like* a noble man, perhaps, but not a noble man). But there are other useful passages dealing with manhood that do not employ this particular term, including direct admonitions by Confucius to his disciples – none of whom, similarly, are thought to have been female.

Let us begin with Confucius's miniature autobiography in *Analects* 2.4; this is his own story of how he became a man:

> The Master said: "At fifteen, I made learning my aspiration. At thirty, I was established. At forty, I was not deluded. At fifty, I knew Heaven's Mandate. At sixty, my ear was compliant. At seventy, I could follow the desires of my heart without overstepping the bounds."

Of these life stages, the first usually receives the least amount of attention in the commentarial literature (both Chinese and English): making learning one's aspiration. But the placement of this stage at the very beginning implies that true manhood is attained only after one adopts learning as one's lifelong quest; yet however rudimentary, this is a prerequisite that most men never fulfil.

Other passages in the *Analects* echo this emphasis on learning:

> The Master said: "The noble man does not seek satiety in his food or security in his dwelling. He is scrupulous in his affairs and careful in his speech. Drawing near to those who possess the Way in order to be corrected by them can be called loving learning." (1.14)

> The Master said: "In a village of ten households there are surely some who are as dutiful or trustworthy as I, but none with the same love of learning." (5.27)

> The Master said: "If I could gain many more years, and used fifty of them for learning, I could indeed be without great faults." (7.17)

> The Master said: "Those born after us are to be held in awe; how do we know that those who come after us will not be the equal of those [active] today? Only someone who is forty or fifty and has still not heard anything [in all those years] is unworthy of being held in awe." (9.23)

The specific value of learning is not always transparent – at times Confucius speaks of learning as an intrinsic and thus unquestioned good – but these passages shed at least some light on Confucius's reasons for treasuring learning: learning makes us better people by improving our conduct and helping us avoid error.

Learning, of course, means more than simply studying books; learning helps us match our statements to our conduct. This is another crucial attribute of the Confucian noble man: he must live up to his words, and is, for that reason, careful about his speech:

> Zigong asked about the noble man. The Master said: "He first advances his views, and then abides by them." (2.13)

> The Master said: "The ancients did not speak profusely; they would be ashamed if they did not measure up [to their words]." (4.22)

> The Master said: "The noble man desires to be slow in speech and scrupulous in action." (4.24)

> The Master said: "At first, when I dealt with people, I would listen to their words and then trust that their actions [would correspond]. Now when I deal with people, I listen to their words and then observe their actions." (5.9)

One of the most succinct statements of this conviction appears in 11.6: "Nan Rong repeatedly recited [the ode about] the white tablet. Confucius gave his niece to him in marriage." The ode in question is Mao 256: "A flaw in the white tablet/can still be polished out;/a flaw in these words of mine/can never be undone." A man like Nan Rong, who knows this principle, and furthermore knows how to convey it to others through elegant citation of classical poetry, is worth bringing into one's family.

What else distinguishes the noble man? Since he has set his heart on learning, he avoids profit-seeking, not because learning and wealth are mutually exclusive, but because *seeking* wealth takes time and energy away from seeking learning. We have seen this attitude already in 1.14 ("The noble man does not seek satiety in his food or security in his dwelling"), and it is frequently repeated: "A man-of-service who has made the Way his aspiration, but who is ashamed of having bad clothing and food, is not worth engaging in discussion" (4.9), and "The noble man is persuaded by righteousness; the petty man is persuaded by profit" (4.16).

A gentleman avoids dogmatism and rigidity; instead, he assesses each situation anew and modifies his conduct accordingly. When in a lofty station, he is kind to his inferiors; when in a position of servitude, he is respectful (though not obsequious).

> The Master said: "One who is not generous when occupying a superior position, or who is not respectful when performing a ritual, or who does not grieve when overseeing mourning rites – how could I bear to look upon such a person?"
> (3.26)

> The Master said of Zichan: "He possessed the Way of the noble man in four respects: he conducted himself with reverence; he served his superiors with respect; he nourished the people with grace; and he employed the people with righteousness." (5.15)

This acquired skill – acting in the right way at the right time – renders the noble man uniquely liberated from anxiety: because he responds to each situation without leaving himself open to reproach, he is always at ease.

> The Master said: "The noble man is relaxed and poised; the petty man is full of agitation." (7.36)

> Sima Niu 司馬牛 [i.e. Sima Geng 司馬耕, d. 481 BCE] asked about the noble man. The Master said: "The noble man does not worry and does not fear".
> [Sima] said: "One who does not worry or fear – is this all that is meant by a noble man?"
> The Master said: "If you examine yourself and find no defect, why would you worry or fear?" (12.4)

It should not be surprising, then, that a gentleman also knows how to avoid punishment and disgrace:

> The Master said: "The noble man contemplates virtue; the petty man contemplates territory. The noble man contemplates punishments; the petty contemplates exemptions." (4.11)

> The Master said of Nan Rong: "When the state possesses the Way, he will not be disenfranchised; when the state does not possess the Way, he will avoid punishment or execution". [Confucius] gave his niece to him in marriage. (5.1)

Nan Rong's ability to prosper in good times and avoid disaster in bad times is singled out as a fine quality in an in-law, and thus as an admirable element of masculinity. Other prospective husbands might be stronger or more courageous, but a gentleman like Nan Rong will be able to stand by his family through thick and thin.

The passages considered here naturally do not exhaust the Way of the Confucian noble man, but they are sufficient for some preliminary stocktaking. What is an ideal man? He loves learning, lives up to his words, and thinks about his relationships with others and acts accordingly. These ideals entail few, if any, physical requirements. A tall man can be a man, and so can a short one; a strong man can be a man, and so can a weak one. Indeed, you hardly have to be a man to be a man! This is not, for example, the ideal man of Genghis Khan:

> Man's greatest good fortune is to chase and defeat his enemy, seize his total possessions, leave his married women weeping and wailing, ride his gelding, use the bodies of his women as a nightshirt and support, gazing upon and kissing their rosy breasts, sucking their lips which are as sweet as the berries of their breasts.[4]

Not every man could be Genghis Khan's man, but *only* a man could; one of the non-negotiable requirements is a penis (not to mention a violent and covetous disposition). But I believe anyone, male or female, could live up to the ethical standards of the Confucian noble man, just as anyone, male or female, could also fail to do so.

To conclude, then, with the question that began this appendix: is Confucianism sexist? If it is, it does not have to be.

Notes

Introduction: what Confucianism is and what Confucianism is not

1. Most famous is Wang Chong 王充 (27–*c*.100 CE). See, for example, Nicolas Zufferey, "Pourquoi Wang Chong critique-t-il Confucius?" *Études Chinoises* **14**(1) (1995), 25–54.
2. Some specific examples will be considered in Chapter 5.
3. For example, Ranjoo Seodu Herr, "Is Confucianism Compatible with Care Ethics? A Critique", *Philosophy East and West* **53**(4) (2003), 471: "Confucianism, as the dominant ideology of East Asia for over two millennia, has played a central role in subjugating women under one of the most systemic and prolonged patriarchies in human history."
4. The most penetrating studies of footbinding are by Dorothy Ko: *Cinderella's Sisters: A Revisionist History of Footbinding* (Berkeley, CA: University of California Press, 2005); and her earlier *Teachers of the Inner Chambers: Women and Culture in Seventeenth-Century China* (Stanford, CA: Stanford University Press, 1994), esp. 147–51 and 169–71. See also Wang Ping, *Aching for Beauty: Footbinding in China* (Minneapolis, MN: University of Minnesota Press, 2000; reprinted, New York: Anchor, 2002).
5. This aspect of footbinding is the main subject of Howard S. Levy, *Chinese Footbinding: The History of a Curious Erotic Custom* (New York: W. Rawls, 1966).
6. For example, Walter H. Slote, "Psychocultural Dynamics within the Confucian Family", in *Confucianism and the Family*, Walter H. Slote & George A. DeVos (eds) (Albany, NY: SUNY Press, 1998), 37–51. Much more judicious is Maurice Freedman, *The Study of Chinese Society*, G. William Skinner (ed.) (Stanford, CA: Stanford University Press, 1979).

7. The tribulations of persons without the means (economic or otherwise) to maintain a standard household are related with exceptional erudition and sensitivity in Matthew H. Sommer, *Sex, Law, and Society in Late Imperial China* (Stanford, CA: Stanford University Press, 2000), e.g. 155–6, 255–9.

8. The classic study is Hsiao-tung Fei, *China's Gentry: Essays on Rural–Urban Relations*, Margaret Park Redfield (rev. & ed.) (Chicago, IL: University of Chicago Press, 1953). More recently, see Joseph W. Esherick & Mary Backus Rankin (eds), *Chinese Local Elites and Patterns of Dominance* (Berkeley, CA: University of California Press, 1990).

9. See, for example, D. E. Mungello, *Curious Land: Jesuit Accommodation and the Origins of Sinology* (Wiesbaden: Franz Steiner, 1985; reprinted, Honolulu, HI: University of Hawaii Press, 1989).

10. The most insightful discussion of Ricci remains Paul A. Rule, *K'ung-tzu or Confucius? The Jesuit Interpretation of Confucianism* (Sydney: Allen & Unwin, 1986), esp. 10–69. Lionel M. Jensen, *Manufacturing Confucianism: Chinese Traditions and Universal Civilization* (Durham, NC: Duke University Press, 1997), is louder but less solid. Jensen is best known for his unfounded charge (81–92) that the Jesuits invented the Chinese appellation "Kong fuzi" 孔夫子, Latinized as "Confucius". In fact, "Kong fuzi" is not rare in pre-Ming literature, and is attested – as searchable databases instantly reveal – as early as the Tang: see, for example, Wang Pu 王溥 (922–82), *Tang huiyao* 唐會要 (Shanghai: Guji, 1991), 80.1747 ("Shifa xia" 謚法下, a discussion of posthumous names). (The *Tang huiyao* was compiled in 961 on the basis of original Tang documents.)

11. For example, *The Five "Confucian" Classics* (New Haven, CT: Yale University Press, 2001), 2n.

12. For an illustrative example, see my "Appeals to History in Early Chinese Philosophy and Rhetoric", *Journal of Chinese Philosophy* 35(1) (2008), 83ff.

13. "Traditionalists", proposed by Graham Sanders in *Words Well Put: Visions of Poetic Competence in the Chinese Tradition* (Cambridge, MA: Harvard University Press, 2006), 15 n.1, is vulnerable to the same objection. Buddhists and Daoists could rightly claim to be "traditionalists" too.

14. For an evenhanded consideration of the *ru* controversy, see Nicolas Zufferey, *To the Origins of Confucianism: The Ru in Pre-Qin Times and During the Early Han Dynasty* (Bern: Peter Lang, 2003); also Chen Lai, "'*Ru*': Xunzi's Thoughts on *ru* and Its Significance", Yan Xin (trans.), *Frontiers of Philosophy in China* 4(2) (2009), 157–79.

15. Recent excavations in China have not only uncovered previously unknown Confucian texts that must have enjoyed canonical status in their day – such as *The Five Forms of Conduct* (*Wuxing* 五行), which was found at a tomb from *c.*300 BCE. in Guodian 郭店 and a tomb from 168 BCE at Mawangdui 馬王堆 – but also revealed that certain neglected texts were more revered in the past than they are today – such as *Jet-Black Robes* (*Ziyi* 緇衣), which was transmit-

ted as a chapter in the received *Ritual Records* (*Liji* 禮記), but has now been recovered in different recensions both from Guodian and from the cache of Warring States manuscripts purchased by the Shanghai Museum. For *The Five Forms of Conduct*, see, for example, Scott Cook, "Consummate Artistry and Moral Virtuosity: The 'Wu xing' 五行 Essay and Its Aesthetic", *Chinese Literature: Essays, Articles, Reviews* **22** (2000), 113–46; for *Jet-Black Robes*, Martin Kern, "Quotation and the Confucian Canon in Early Chinese Manuscripts: The Case of 'Zi yi' (Black Robes)", *Asiatische Studien* **59**(1) (2005), 293–332. For a representative Chinese view, see Hu Zhihong, "The Obscuration and Rediscovery of the Original Confucian Thought of Moral Politics: Deciphering Work on the Guodian, Shangbo and the Transmitted Versions of *Ziyi*", Huang Deyuan (trans.), *Frontiers of Philosophy in China* **3**(4) (2008), 535–57.

1. Confucius and his disciples

1. There are various conventions by which the *Analects* are divided into chapter and verse; I follow here the numberings given by James Legge (1815–1897) in *The Chinese Classics*, 2nd edn (Oxford: Clarendon Press, 1893–95; reprinted, Taipei: SMC, 1991), vol. 1. All translations in this book are my own unless otherwise indicated.

2. Edward L. Shaughnessy, *Sources of Western Zhou History: Inscribed Bronze Vessels* (Berkeley, CA: University of California Press, 1991), is a standard introduction to this material.

3. For a *summa* of a lifetime of research in this field, see David N. Keightley, "The Making of the Ancestors: Late Shang Religion and Its Legacy", in *Religion and Chinese Society: A Centennial Conference of the École française d'Extrême-Orient*, John Lagerwey (ed.) (Paris: École française d'Extrême-Orient, 2004), 1, 3–63.

4. Of the various recent studies of the sociology of early Chinese writing, I am most persuaded by Robert W. Bagley, "Anyang Writing and the Origin of the Chinese Writing System", in *The First Writing: Script Invention as History and Process*, Stephen D. Houston (ed.) (Cambridge: Cambridge University Press, 2004), 190–249. For writing in the period immediately preceding Confucius, see Martin Kern, "The Performance of Writing in Western Zhou China", in *The Poetics of Grammar and the Metaphysics of Sound and Sign*, S. La Porta & D. Shulman (eds) (Leiden: Brill, 2007), 109–75.

5. Cf. Sor-hoon Tan, "Three Corners for One: Tradition and Creativity in the *Analects*", in *Confucius Now: Contemporary Encounters with the* Analects, David Jones (ed.) (La Salle, IL: Open Court, 2008), 59–77.

6. *Bo* 柏, "cypress", may have been less popular as a name because of its graphic and phonetic propinquity to *po* 迫, "to oppress". Cf. C. H. Wang, *The Bell and*

the Drum: Shih ching as Formulaic Poetry in an Oral Tradition (Berkeley, CA: University of California Press, 1974), 111.

7. Other traditions alluded to the same properties of evergreens; one of the legendary sages of the Daoist tradition, for example, is the Master of the Red Pine (Chisongzi 赤松子).

8. The best overview is John Makeham, "The Formation of *Lunyu* as a Book", *Monumenta Serica* **44** (1996), 1–24; Wojciech Jan Simson, *Die Geschichte der Aussprüche des Konfuzius (Lunyu)* (Bern: Peter Lang, 2006), attacks most traditional scholarship without submitting many theories of his own.

9. For a fine recent study, see Yuri Pines, "Lexical Changes in Zhanguo Texts", *Journal of the American Oriental Society* **122**(4) (2002), e.g. 697.

10. For example, I do not agree with Tsuda Sōkichi 津田左右吉 (1873–1961), *Rongo to Kōshi no shisō* 論語と孔子の思想 (Tokyo: Iwanami, 1946), who argued that the text is riddled with internal contradictions and therefore cannot be used to reconstruct Confucius's philosophy.

11. See, for example, D. C. Lau, *Confucius: The Analects*, 2nd edn (Hong Kong: Chinese University Press, 1992), 265–75. E. Bruce Brooks & A. Taeko Brooks, *The Original Analects: Sayings of Confucius and His Successors* (New York: Columbia University Press, 1998), go further than this and attempt to date each chapter of the text to a precise year. They lay out the methodology behind their novel dates in Appendix 1, "The Accretion Theory of the Analects", 201–48. Their reasoning is fallacious: while they are correct that different chapters display different themes and styles, they seem to assume that the only way to explain such phenomena is to postulate a unique date of composition for each chapter. Cf. also Benjamin I. Schwartz, *The World of Thought in Ancient China* (Cambridge, MA: Harvard University Press, Belknap Press, 1985), 61f.

12. Despite John Makeham, "Between Chen and Cai: *Zhuangzi* and the *Analects*", in *Wandering at Ease in the* Zhuangzi, Roger T. Ames (ed.) (Albany, NY: SUNY Press, 1998), 75–100; see my review in *Journal of the American Oriental Society* **120**(3) (2000), 475–6. See also Ronnie Littlejohn, "Kongzi in the *Zhuangzi*", in *Experimental Essays on Zhuangzi*, 2nd edn, Victor H. Mair (ed.) (Dunedin, FL: Three Pines, 2010), 177–94.

13. Useful treatments of Confucius's life include Mark Csikszentmihalyi, "Confucius", in *The Rivers of Paradise: Moses, Buddha, Confucius, Jesus, and Muhammad as Religious Founders*, David Noel Freedman & Michael J. McClymond (eds) (Grand Rapids, MI: Eerdmans, 2001), 233–308; Jean Lévi, *Confucius* (Paris: Pygmalion/Gérard Watelet, 2002); Heiner Roetz, *Konfuzius*, 2nd edn (Munich: C. H. Beck, 1998); Shigeki Kaizuka, *Confucius: His Life and Thought*, Geoffrey Bownas (trans.) (London: Allen & Unwin, 1956); H. G. Creel, *Confucius and the Chinese Way* (reprinted, New York: Harper & Row, 1960), esp. 25–172; and Richard Wilhelm, *Confucius and Confucianism*, George H. Danton & Annina Periam Danton (trans.) (New York: Harcourt Brace Jovanovich, 1931), 3–95.

14. On this process, see esp. Lionel M. Jensen, "Wise Man of the Wilds: Father-lessness, Fertility, and the Mythic Exemplar, Kongzi", *Early China* 20 (1995): 407–37; and *idem*, "The Genesis of Kongzi in Ancient Narrative: The Figura-tive as Historical", in *On Sacred Grounds: Culture, Society, Politics, and the Formation of the Cult of Confucius*, Thomas A. Wilson (ed.) (Cambridge, MA: Harvard University Press, 2002), 175–221; also Mark Csikszentmiha-lyi, "Confucius and the *Analects* in the Hàn", in *Confucius and the* Analects: *New Essays*, Bryan W. Van Norden (ed.) (Oxford: Oxford University Press, 2002), e.g. 136–44. The changing conceptions of Confucius after his death are explored in Michael Nylan & Thomas Wilson, *Lives of Confucius: Civilization's Greatest Sage through the Ages* (New York: Doubleday, 2010).

15. For an overview of the problems and some ingenious, if speculative, sugges-tions, see Robert Eno, "The Background of the Kong Family of Lu and the Origins of Ruism", *Early China* 28 (2003), 1–41.

16. Cf. "The Master said: 'The Way is not distant from human beings. If people practice the Way so as to make it distant from human beings, they cannot be practicing the Way'" (*Zhongyong* 中庸 13). Tu Wei-ming has emphasized the notion of the Confucian "fiduciary community" in several publications, most notably *Centrality and Commonality: An Essay on Confucian Religiousness* (Albany, NY: SUNY Press, 1989), 39–66.

17. *Zhongyong* 16 emphasizes the power of the spirits and the importance of remembering them in the midst of ritual performance.

18. The secondary literature on *shu* and the "one thing with which to string eve-rything together" is enormous. See, for example, Herbert Fingarette, "Follow-ing the 'One Thread' of the *Analects*", in *Studies in Classical Chinese Thought*, Henry Rosemont, Jr & Benjamin I. Schwartz (eds), *Journal of the American Academy of Religion* 47(3), *Thematic Issue* S (1979), 373–405; H. G. Creel, "Discussion of Professor Fingarette on Confucius", in *Studies in Classical Chi-nese Thought*, Rosemont & Schwartz, 407–15; David S. Nivison, *The Ways of Confucianism: Investigations in Chinese Philosophy*, Bryan W. Van Norden (ed.) (Chicago, IL: Open Court, 1996), 59–76; Sin Yee Chan, "Disputes on the One Thread of *Chung-Shu*", *Journal of Chinese Philosophy* 26(2) (1999), 165–86; Bryan W. Van Norden, "Unweaving the 'One Thread' of *Analects* 4:15", in *Confucius and the* Analects, Van Norden (ed.), 216–36; Bo Mou, "A Reex-amination of the Structure and Content of Confucius' Version of the Golden Rule", *Philosophy East and West* 54(2) (2004), 218–48; and Philip J. Ivanhoe, "The 'Golden Rule' in the *Analects*", in *Confucius Now*, Jones (ed.), 81–107. I do not see any reason to follow Van Norden's argument that *Analects* 4.15 is an interpolation.

19. Martha Nussbaum seems to sense this problem: "The Chinese forms [of the Golden Rule] do not say, 'Treat another as you would have that other treat you,' but 'Treat another as you would have anyone else related to you as you are related to that other treat you'" ("Golden Rule Arguments: A Missing

Thought?" in *The Moral Circle and the Self: Chinese and Western Approaches*, Kim-chong Chong *et al.* [eds] [La Salle, IL: Open Court, 2003], esp. 6).

20. Cf. my "The Theme of the Primacy of the Situation in Classical Chinese Philosophy and Rhetoric", *Asia Major* (3rd series) **18**(2) (2005), 1ff.
21. Alan Gewirth has considered these problems in "The Golden Rule Rationalized", *Midwest Studies in Philosophy* **3** (1978), 133–47, and *Reason and Morality* (Chicago, IL: University of Chicago Press, 1981).
22. Lau, *Confucius*, 33.
23. See the fuller defence in my "When *Zhong* 忠 Does Not Mean 'Loyalty,'" *Dao* **7**(2) (2008), esp. 168–70.
24. The modern understanding of this connection goes back to Peter A. Boodberg; see *Selected Works of Peter A. Boodberg*, Alvin P. Cohen (ed.) (Berkeley, CA: University of California Press, 1979), 36ff. On paronomasia in the *Analects* generally, see Roger T. Ames, "Paronomasia: A Confucian Way of Making Meaning", in *Confucius Now*, Jones (ed.), 37–48.
25. A rhetorical question intended to convey that the practice of humanity surely emerges from the self, and does not depend on others.
26. For example, Herbert Fingarette, *Confucius: The Secular as Sacred* (New York: Harper & Row, 1972), 9ff., discusses the convention of shaking hands as an example of *li* (which would make Confucius something like a tacit contractarian), but this is inadequate from a Confucian point of view because shaking hands is not in and of itself conducive to moral self-cultivation. Even tyrants know how to shake hands in a socially acceptable manner. As we shall see in Chapter 4, the question of whether the rites can be arbitrarily constructed and retain their effectiveness became an important one in Chinese philosophy, and the Confucian view was always the same: *li* can only be conventions that facilitate social interaction *while also* inducing its performers to improve themselves morally. Social cohesion is not a sufficient goal *per se*.
27. The first two lines (though not the third line) are found in Mao 57, a poem in the *Odes*.
28. Cf. my *After Confucius: Studies in Early Chinese Philosophy* (Honolulu, HI: University of Hawaii Press, 2005), 19–35.
29. I do not find this interpretation of *li* elsewhere in the secondary literature. The nearest alternative view is probably that of Kwong-loi Shun, "*Rén* 仁 and *Lǐ* 禮 in the *Analects*", in *Confucius and the* Analects, Van Norden (ed.), 53–72; see also Karyn Lai, "*Li* in the *Analects*: Training in Moral Competence and the Question of Flexibility", *Philosophy East and West* **56**(1) (2006), 69–83.
30. See further Schwartz, *The World of Thought in Ancient China*, 103.
31. Cf. *Mencius* 1B.8, where the slaughter of the tyrants Jie 桀 and Zhòu 紂 is sanctioned on the grounds that they were not true kings.
32. I do not consider here the very different argument for rectifying names in *Analects* 13.3, since there are longstanding doubts about its authenticity. For

the reasons, see Arthur Waley, *The Analects of Confucius* (London: Allen & Unwin, 1938), 21–2, 172 n.1; and Creel, *Confucius and the Chinese Way*, 321 n.13. For an insightful interpretation by a scholar who takes it straight, see Hui-chieh Loy, "*Analects* 13.3 and the Doctrine of 'Correcting Names,'" in *Confucius Now*, Jones (ed.), 223–42.

33. Other philosophers, such as those interested in logic, would go on to use non-moral criteria to determine appropriate names. The best study remains A. C. Graham, *Later Mohist Logic, Ethics and Science* (Hong Kong: Chinese University Press, 1978), esp. 25–72, but for an important methodological criticism of this book, see Jane M. Geaney, "A Critique of A. C. Graham's Reconstruction of the 'Neo-Mohist Canons,'" *Journal of the American Oriental Society* **119**(1) (1999), 1–11.

34. Cf. Cho-yun Hsu, *Ancient China in Transition: An Analysis of Social Mobility, 722–222 BC* (Stanford, CA: Stanford University Press, 1965), 158ff.; see also Robert H. Gassmann, "Die Bezeichnung *jun-zi*: Ansätze zur Chun-qiu-zeitlichen Kontextualisierung und zur Bedeutungsbestimmung im *Lun Yu*", in *Zurück zur Freude: Studien zur chinesichen Literatur und Lebenswelt und ihrer Rezeption in Ost und West: Festschrift für Wolfgang Kubin*, Marc Hermann & Christian Schwermann (eds) (Sankt Augustin: Steyler Verlag, 2007), 411–36.

35. See the Appendix.

36. The relevant bibliography is extensive; for my own view, see my *The Culture of Sex in Ancient China* (Honolulu, HI: University of Hawaii Press, 2002), 55ff.

37. Cf. "The noble man acts as befits his station and does not yearn for anything beyond it. When in wealth and nobility, he acts in accordance with his wealth and nobility; when in poverty and ignobility, he acts in accordance with his poverty and ignobility; when among barbarians, he acts in accordance with his being among barbarians; when in straits and difficulty, he acts in accordance with his straits and difficulty. There is no place that the noble man enters where he does not find himself" (*Zhongyong* 14).

38. The name can also be taken to mean "Self-Righteous". Cf. Goldin, *After Confucius*, 8.

39. See, for example, Grant Hardy, *Worlds of Bronze and Bamboo: Sima Qian's Conquest of History* (New York: Columbia University Press, 1999), 199f.

40. For example, *Analects* 1.16: "The Master said: 'I am not vexed at others' not knowing me; I am vexed at not knowing others.'"

41. Cf. U. Hattori, "Confucius' Conviction of His Heavenly Mission", S. Elisséeff (trans.), *Harvard Journal of Asiatic Studies* **1**(1) (1936), 96–108.

42. "The Master said: 'At fifteen, I made learning my aspiration. At thirty, I was established. At forty, I was not deluded. At fifty, I knew Heaven's Mandate. At sixty, my ear was compliant. At seventy, I could follow the desires of my heart without overstepping the bounds'" (*Analects* 2.4).

2. Interlude: *Great Learning* and *Canon of Filial Piety*

1. The last sentence is unclear and has been the subject of much commentarial dispute. The penultimate sentence is more comprehensible: the idea is that one cannot expect to have an orderly state and family if one does not first cultivate oneself.

2. This is a quote from Mao 235.

3. The classic text in this vein is *Discourses on Salt and Iron* (*Yantie lun* 鹽鉄論). For partial translations of this text, see Esson M. Gale, *Discourses on Salt and Iron: A Debate on State Control of Commerce and Industry in Ancient China*, (Leiden: Brill, 1931); Esson M. Gale *et al.*, "Discourses on Salt and Iron [*Yen T'ieh Lun*: Chaps. XX–XXVIII]", *Journal of the North China Branch of the Royal Asiatic Society* 65 (1934), 73–110; and Sabine Ludwig, "Huan Kuan, Yantie lun: Die Debatte über Salz und Eisen", Erling von Mende (ed.), in *Vademecum zu dem Klassiker der chinesischen Wirtschaftsdebatten*, Bertram Schefold (ed.) (Düsseldorf: Handelsblatt, 2002), 107–83.

4. Several articles in the recent volume *Filial Piety in Chinese Thought and History*, Alan K. L. Chan & Sor-hoon Tan (eds) (London: Routledge Curzon, 2004), address non-Confucian understandings of *xiao*: Ikeda Tomohisa, "The Evolution of the Concept of Filial Piety (*xiao*) in the *Laozi*, the *Zhuangzi*, and the Guodian Bamboo Text *Yucong*", 12–28; Yuet Keung Lo, "Filial Devotion for Women: A Buddhist Testimony from Third-Century China", 71–90; Livia Kohn, "Immortal Parents and Universal Kin: Family Values in Medieval Daoism", 91–109; Mugitani Kunio, "Filial Piety and 'Authentic Parents' in Religious Daoism", 110–21. See also my review of the book in *Dao* 5(2) (2006), 371–75.

5. The fullest study in any language is Ikezawa Masaru 池澤優, *"Kō" shisō no shūkyōgakuteki kenkyū: Kodai Chūgoku ni okeru sosen sūhai no shisōteki hatten*「孝」思想の宗教学的研究:古代中国における祖先崇拝の思想的発展 (Tokyo: Tōkyō Daigaku Shuppankai, 2002). In English, see esp. Keith N. Knapp, "The *Ru* Reinterpretation of *Xiao*", *Early China* 20 (1995), 195–222; also Donald Holzman, "The Place of Filial Piety in Ancient China", *Journal of the American Oriental Society* 118(2) (1998), 185–99; Harry Hsin-i Hsiao, "A Preliminary Interpretation of the Origin of the Concept of *hsiao* in the Shang Period", *Chinese Culture* 19(3) (1978), 5–20, and "Concepts of *hsiao* in the *Classic of Poetry* and the *Classic of Documents*", *Journal of the Institute of Chinese Studies of the Chinese University of Hong Kong* 10(2) (1979), 425–43.

6. For example, for Bertrand Russell (1872–1970), "Filial piety, and the strength of the family generally, are perhaps the weakest point in Confucian ethics, the only point where the system departs seriously from common sense" (*The Problem of China* [London: Allen & Unwin, 1922], 40).

7. Cf. Anne Behnke Kinney, *Representations of Childhood and Youth in Early China* (Stanford, CA: Stanford University Press, 2004), 26–7.

8. A play on words: the character for "instruction" (*jiao* 教) contains the character for "filial piety" (*xiao* 孝) as a graphic element. A close relationship was presumed between the two concepts.

9. This is another quote from Mao 235. The text could be taken to mean "your virtue" or "their virtue", and this ambiguity is fitting: by cultivating one's own virtue, one is also perpetuating that of one's ancestors.

10. To be fair, Wu said that this was "the great application of filial piety" 孝字的大作用, not necessarily the original meaning. See "Shuo xiao" 説孝, in *Wu Yu wenlu* 吳虞文錄, 2nd edn (Shanghai: Yadong tushuguan, 1922), 15; the translation above is from Chow Tse-tsung, *The May Fourth Movement: Intellectual Revolution in Modern China* (Cambridge, MA: Harvard University Press, 1960), 304. Chow discusses Wu Yu and anti-Confucianism further in "The Anti-Confucian Movement in Early Republican China", in *The Confucian Persuasion*, Arthur F. Wright (ed.) (Stanford, CA: Stanford University Press, 1960), 288–312.

11. The metaphor refers to a warp-weighted loom.

12. This is a quote from Mao 191. Master Yin is usually taken to be a minister of state.

3. Mencius

1. D. C. Lau surveys the surviving references in *Mencius: A Bilingual Edition*, rev. edn (Hong Kong: Chinese University Press, 2003), 332–40.

2. On *quan*, see Goldin, "The Theme of the Primacy of the Situation", esp. 19ff.; and Griet Vankeerberghen, "Choosing Balance: Weighing (*quan*) as a Metaphor for Action in Early Chinese Texts", *Early China* 30 (2005–6), 47–89.

3. The original is confusing here and may be garbled. Presumably Mencius means that one must make it one's constant duty to nourish one's "flood-like *qi*".

4. Cf. Alan K. L. Chan, "A Matter of Taste: *Qi* (Vital Energy) and the Tending of the Heart (*Xin*) in *Mencius* 2A.2", in *Mencius: Contexts and Interpretations*, Alan K. L. Chan (ed.) (Honolulu, HI: University of Hawaii Press, 2002), 42–71, although I think that by rendering *qi* questionably as "vital energy" Chan causes himself to miss the obvious inference that Mencius was alluding to contemporary concepts of physical self-cultivation. See, for example, Michael J. Puett, *To Become a God: Cosmology, Sacrifice, and Self-Divinization in Early China* (Cambridge, MA: Harvard University Press, 2002), 134; also Lee Rainey, "Mencius and His Vast, Overflowing *qi* (*haoran zhi qi*)", *Monumenta Serica* 46 (1998), 91–104.

5. See my review of A. C. Graham (trans.), *Chuang-tzu: The Inner Chapters*, and Harold D. Roth, *A Companion to Angus C. Graham's Chuang-tzu: The Inner Chapters*, in *Early China* 28 (2003), 204ff. Western-trained philosophers

sometimes depict Yang Zhu as a Chinese egoist, and turn him into a more influential figure than he really was. An informed recent treatment is Erica Fox Brindley, *Individualism in Early China: Human Agency and the Self in Thought and Politics* (Honolulu, HI: University of Hawaii Press, 2010), 70–76.

6. The first substantial study of Mencius's exchange with Yi Zhi was Nivison, *The Ways of Confucianism*, 133–48. See also Bryan W. Van Norden, *Virtue Ethics and Consequentialism in Early Chinese Philosophy* (Cambridge: Cambridge University Press, 2007), 305ff.; and Kwong-loi Shun, *Mencius and Early Chinese Thought* (Stanford, CA: Stanford University Press, 1997), 127–35.

7. For Confucius and Mencius, I have translated *xin* 心 as "heart", bearing in mind the observation of Irene Bloom, "On the Matter of the Mind: The Metaphysical Basis of the Expanded Self", in *Individualism and Holism: Studies in Confucian and Taoist Values*, Donald J. Munro (ed.) (Ann Arbor, MI: University of Michigan Center for Chinese Studies, 1985), 300, that the associations of the word "were visceral rather than cerebral". For Xunzi, however, as we shall see, "heart" no longer captures all the dimensions of *xin*.

8. Cf. "That by which people are different from birds and beasts is slight. Common people abandon it; the noble man preserves it" (*Mencius* 4B.19:) and "That by which the noble man is different from other people is his preservation of his heart" (4B.28).

9. See, for example, Van Norden, *Virtue Ethics and Consequentialism in Early Chinese Philosophy*, 234–46; also Philip J. Ivanhoe, "Confucian Self-Cultivation and Mengzi's Notion of Extension", in *Essays on the Moral Philosophy of Mengzi*, Xiusheng Liu & Philip J. Ivanhoe (eds) (Indianapolis, IN: Hackett, 2002), 221–41.

10. Cf. also *Mencius* 7B.31.

11. A. C. Graham, *Studies in Chinese Philosophy and Philosophical Literature* (Albany, NY: SUNY Press, 1990), 7–66; see also his *Disputers of the Tao: Philosophical Argument in Ancient China* (La Salle, IL: Open Court, 1989), 117–32.

12. The fullest discussion is now Van Norden, *Virtue Ethics and Consequentialism in Early Chinese Philosophy*, 225ff., 278–301; see also Shun, *Mencius and Early Chinese Thought*, 210–22.

13. Nivison, *The Ways of Confucianism*, 150–52, struggles with it too.

14. This point has been most forcefully articulated by Roger T. Ames in, for example, "The Mencian Conception of *Ren xing* 人性: Does It Mean 'Human Nature'?" in *Chinese Texts and Philosophical Contexts: Essays Dedicated to Angus C. Graham*, Henry Rosemont, Jr (ed.) (La Salle, IL: Open Court, 1991), 143–75. See also Irene Bloom, "Mencian Arguments on Human Nature (*Jen-hsing*)", *Philosophy East and West* 44(1) (1994), 19–53. Ames is most persuasive when he stays close to Mencius; he errs, in my opinion, when he begins to argue as though Mencius's conception of *xing* were valid for all Confucians: for example, "Whatever Happened to 'Wisdom'? Confucian Philosophy of Process and 'Human Becomings'", *Asia Major* (3rd series) 21(1) (2008), 45–68.

15. Literally, "by the days' nights", but clearly the night-time, when the lumberjacks are not assailing the mountain, is intended here.

16. Literally, "by the days' nights", as above.

17. The Chinese word is *cai* 才, which is related to the word that Mencius used above to refer to the "timber" (*cai* 材) on Ox Mountain. This paronomasia is intentional.

18. Cf. "A footpath in the mountains, if it is used steadfastly, will become a road, but if it is not used for a while, it will be blocked by weeds. Now weeds are blocking your heart" (*Mencius* 7B.21).

19. Oscar Wilde (1854–1900), *The Importance of Being Earnest*, in *Complete Works of Oscar Wilde* (London: Collins, 1966), 330.

20. Thus I do not fully agree with the accounts in Shun, *Mencius and Early Chinese Thought*, 77–83; and Ning Chen, "The Concept of Fate in *Mencius*", *Philosophy East and West* **47**(4) (1997), 495–520.

21. Cf. also *Mencius* 1A.2.

22. Mao 250; the received text is slightly different.

23. Mao 237.

24. Cf. Michael Nylan, with Harrison Huang, "Mencius on Pleasure", in *Polishing the Chinese Mirror: Essays in Honor of Henry Rosemont, Jr.*, Marthe Chandler & Ronnie Littlejohn (eds) (New York: Global Scholarly Publications, 2008), 253ff.

25. Cf. Antonio S. Cua, *Human Nature, Ritual, and History: Studies in Xunzi and Chinese Philosophy* (Washington, DC: Catholic University of America Press, 2005), 354–68.

26. This is a unit of distance roughly equivalent to one-third of a mile.

27. That is to say, the regicides already possess one-tenth of their state's total number of chariots.

28. Neo-Confucians such as Cheng Yi 程頤 (1033–1107) and Zhu Xi 朱熹 (1130–1200), commenting on this passage, observed that humanity and righteousness are profitable in their own right. See Zhu Xi, *Sishu zhangju jizhu* 四書章句集注, Xu Deming 徐德明 (ed.) (Shanghai: Guji, 2001), 235. Cf. Carine Defoort, "The Profit That Does Not Profit: Paradoxes with *li* in Early Chinese Texts", *Asia Major* (3rd series) **21**(1) (2008), 168.

29. Cf. also *Mencius* 4A.8.

30. Cf. also *Mencius* 1A.3, 1A.5, 7A.22–23.

31. For example, Chun-chieh Huang, *Mencian Hermeneutics: A History of Interpretations in China* (New Brunswick, NJ: Transaction, 2001), 249.

32. See my "Hsiao Kung-chuan on Mencian Populism", in *Xiao Gongquan xueji* 蕭公權學記, Wang Rongzu 汪榮祖 & Huang Junjie 黃俊傑 (eds) (Taipei: National Taiwan University Press, 2009), 249–63; and Justin Tiwald, "A Right of Rebellion in the *Mengzi*?" *Dao* **7**(3) (2008), 269–82.

33. Cf. Yuri Pines, "Disputers of Abdication: Zhanguo Egalitarianism and the Sovereign's Power", *T'oung Pao* **91**(4–5) (2005), 275ff.

34. Cf. Graham, *Disputers of the Tao*, 113.

35. Mao 244.

36. There are many other passages advancing the same general claim, for example, *Mencius* 1A.5–7, 1B.10–11, 2A.5, 3B.5.

4. Xunzi

1. The source of this oft-repeated phrase is "Mengzi Xun Qing liezhuan" 孟子荀卿列傳, *Shiji* 史記 (Beijing: Zhonghua, 1959), 74.2348.

2. This is stated in the preface by Liu Xiang 劉向, conveniently included in Wang Xianqian 王先謙 (1842–1918), *Xunzi jijie* 荀子集解, Shen Xiaohuan 沈嘯寰 & Wang Xingxian 王星賢 (eds) (Beijing: Zhonghua, 1988), 558.

3. On the rise of Mencianism in this period, see Wolfgang Ommerborn, "Einflüsse des Menzius und seiner Theorie der Politik der Menschlichkeit (*renzheng*) in der Zeit vom 3. Jh. bis zum Ende der Tang-Zeit", *Archiv Orientální* 73 (2005), 111–39.

4. Han Yu 韓愈, "Du Xun" 讀荀, *Han Changli wenji jiaozhu* 韓昌黎文集校注, Ma Tongbo 馬通伯 (ed.) (Beijing: Zhonghua, 1972), 1.20–21, translated in Charles Hartman, *Han Yü and the T'ang Search for Unity* (Princeton, NJ: Princeton University Press, 1986), 181–2

5. Zhu Xi's fullest exposition of his distaste for Xunzi appears in the preface to his commentary on the poem "Chengxiang" 成相 in *Chuci houyu* 楚辭後語 (*Siku quanshu* 四庫全書), 1.1a–2a. See also Li Jingde 黎靖德 (fl. 1263), *Zhuzi yulei* 朱子語類, Wang Xingxian (ed.) (Beijing: Zhonghua, 1985), 137.3255. It is, of course, possible that Song Neo-Confucians were deeply indebted to Xunzi even as they excoriated him. See, for example, Don J. Wyatt, *The Recluse of Loyang: Shao Yung and the Moral Evolution of Early Sung Thought* (Honolulu, HI: University of Hawaii Press, 1996), 83–4, 177.

6. For the important exception of Ling Tingkan 凌廷堪 (1755–1809), see Kai-wing Chow, *The Rise of Confucian Ritualism in Late Imperial China: Ethics, Classics, and Lineage Discourse* (Stanford, CA: Stanford University Press, 1994), 191–7.

7. See Kung-chuan Hsiao, *A Modern China and a New World: K'ang Yu-wei, Reformer and Utopian, 1858–1927* (Seattle, WA: University of Washington Press, 1975), 46–7, 79.

8. Tan laid out his objections to Xunzi in §§29 and 30 of his *Renxue* 仁學; see the bilingual edition by Chan Sin-wai, *An Exposition of Benevolence: The Jen-hsüeh of T'an Ssu-t'ung* (Hong Kong: Chinese University Press, 1984), 146–52 (English), 270–72 (Chinese). Cf. also Carsun Chang, *The Development of Neo-Confucian Thought* (New York: Bookman, 1957–62), II, 423–4.

9. See Hao Chang, *Liang Ch'i-ch'ao and Intellectual Transition in China, 1890–1907* (Cambridge, MA: Harvard University Press, 1971), 74ff.; Carsun Chang, *The Development of Neo-Confucian Thought*, II, 425; and Joseph R. Levenson,

Liang Ch'i-ch'ao and the Mind of Modern China, rev. edn (Cambridge, MA: Harvard University Press, 1959), 35.

10. Kam Louie, *Inheriting Tradition: Interpretations of the Classical Philosophers in Communist China, 1949–1966* (Oxford: Oxford University Press, 1986), 165–78, shows that the rehabilitation of Xunzi (along ideological lines) was already well underway during the first two decades of the People's Republic.

11. Since 1999 alone: my *Rituals of the Way: The Philosophy of Xunzi* (La Salle, IL: Open Court, 1999); T. C. Kline III & Philip J. Ivanhoe (eds), *Virtue, Nature, and Moral Agency in the* Xunzi (Indianapolis, IN: Hackett, 2000); Masayuki Sato, *The Confucian Quest for Order: The Origin and Formation of the Political Thought of Xun Zi* (Leiden: Brill, 2003); Cua, *Human Nature, Ritual, and History*; Janghee Lee, *Xunzi and Early Chinese Naturalism* (Albany, NY: SUNY Press, 2005); Kurtis Hagen, *The Philosophy of Xunzi: A Reconstruction* (La Salle, IL: Open Court, 2006); and Aaron Stalnaker, *Overcoming Our Evil: Human Nature and Spiritual Exercises in Xunzi and Augustine* (Washington, DC: Georgetown University Press, 2006).

12. The above overview of Xunzi's reception over the centuries is borrowed from my "Xunzi and Early Han Philosophy", *Harvard Journal of Asiatic Studies* **67**(1) (2007), 135–6.

13. For the alternation between the surnames Sun 孫 and Xun 荀, see Goldin, *Rituals of the Way*, 108 n.1; and John Knoblock (trans.), *Xunzi: A Translation and Study of the Complete Works* (Stanford, CA: Stanford University Press, 1988–1994), I, 234ff.

14. See Sato, *The Confucian Quest for Order*, 27–36, for a solid overview of the textual history.

15. Cf., generally, Mark Edward Lewis, *Writing and Authority in Early China* (Albany, NY: SUNY Press, 1999), 62–3.

16. For an overview of how the following account of Xunzi's philosophy differs from my earlier *Rituals of the Way*, see my "Response: Xunzi, Again", in *Dao* **5**(1) (2005), 204–6.

17. For a lucid overview, see Eric Hutton, "Does Xunzi Have a Consistent Theory of Human Nature?" in *Virtue, Nature, and Moral Agency in the* Xunzi, Kline & Ivanhoe (eds), 220–36; also Goldin, *Rituals of the Way*, 6ff.

18. Since there is no universally recognized citation system for passages in *Xunzi*, I shall use the section numbers in Knoblock. My translations, however, will often diverge from those of Knoblock substantially.

19. See also *Xunzi* 22.5b.

20. Cf. also *Xunzi* 8.11.

21. Graham, *Disputers of the Tao*, 250. See also Shun, *Mencius and Early Chinese Thought*, 222–31.

22. For an example of this view, see Patricia Buckley Ebrey, *Confucianism and Family Rituals in Imperial China: A Social History of Writing about Rites* (Princeton, NJ: Princeton University Press, 1991), 26ff.

23. Cf. Goldin, *Rituals of the Way*, 71ff.

24. Compare also *Xunzi* 10.3a, 19.1c.

25. These accoutrements are prescribed by *Vestments of Mourning* (*Sangfu* 喪服), an ancient document currently found in the canonical collection called *Ceremonies and Rites* (*Yili* 儀禮), and the explanatory phrase "hatband and waistband" is here supplied on the basis of that text. Other commentarial explanations of *ju zhang* 苴杖 ("female nettle plant and staff") in this instance strike me as less convincing.

26. This statement is difficult to construe, and there is a conspicuous lack of commentary about it. Perhaps Xunzi means to say that music ("sounds and tones, movement and quietude") is a technique for improving the *xing* and thus fulfilling the Way of Humanity. This would be in line with his general views.

27. The original is unclear here.

28. Cf. "All those who say that order depends on eliminating desires have no means of guiding desires, and thus are distressed that they have any desires at all. All those who say that order depends on reducing desires have no means of moderating desires, and thus are distressed that their desires are so many" (*Xunzi* 22.5a).

29. Cf. Goldin, *Rituals of the Way*, 77ff.

30. Cf. Scott Cook, "Xun Zi on Ritual and Music", *Monumenta Serica* 45 (1997), 21ff.; and Graham, *Disputers of the Tao*, 259ff.

31. "Procedures of the Officials" sounds like the title of an authoritative text of some kind, but Xunzi is actually quoting his own words from a different essay.

32. By "Elegantiae" (*ya* 雅) Xunzi may mean either the section of the canonical *Odes* by that name, or the "elegant" music sanctioned by the sages – or both, since these alternatives amount to essentially the same thing.

33. See Goldin, *Rituals of the Way*, 98ff.; also Goldin, *After Confucius*, 42ff., for recently discovered Confucian antecedents to Xunzi's use of the Way.

34. Schwartz, *The World of Thought in Ancient China*, 62ff., interprets Confucius's "Way" as the equivalent of a "good system", but the word "system" sounds a false note, inasmuch as Confucius cannot be plausibly categorized as a systematic philosopher.

35. Or conceivably "for the way [you have chosen] is such" (*qi dao ran* 其道然).

36. Xunzi borrows this term from the *Zhuangzi* 莊子, where it refers to those rare people who dispense with the mundane distinctions of the social world in order to embrace the incalculably greater benefits of living in accord with the Way. See, above all, Judith Berling, "Self and Whole in Chuang Tzu", in Munro, *Individualism and Holism*, 101–20; also Eske Møllgaard, *An Introduction to Daoist Thought: Action, Language, and Ethics in Zhuangzi* (London: Routledge, 2007), 15–20. Xunzi attempts here to give a more Confucian understanding of the concept.

37. Hagen, *The Philosophy of Xunzi*, 17–40. For a similar example, see Lee, *Xunzi and Early Chinese Naturalism*, 71ff. Both Hagen and Lee, it should be noted, are former students of Roger T. Ames, but I suspect that the primary inspiration for such interpretations is Graham's terse discussion in *Disputers of the Tao*, 243, beginning with: "Is Xunzi saying that man imposes his own meaning on an otherwise meaningless universe? He is very near to this modern idea" (with romanization converted). Graham went on to explain why this reading would be unfounded, however. For Ames's treatment of Xunzi, see David L. Hall & Roger T. Ames, *Anticipating China: Thinking through the Narratives of Chinese and Western Culture* (Albany, NY: SUNY Press, 1995), 202–11.

38. For notes on this difficult passage, see Goldin, "The Theme of the Primacy of the Situation", 25 n.72. Compare *Xunzi* 5.5: "In antiquity and the present day, there is but one measure. Categories do not diverge; however much time has passed, the patterns are the same".

39. That is, (i) lack of separation between internal and external, male and female; (ii) friction between father and son, superior and inferior; and (iii) crime and hardship.

40. Cf. Goldin, *Rituals of the Way*, 47ff. Xunzi's idea of "human portents" is adumbrated in *Mencius* 2A.4 and 4A.8, which attribute the same lines to a text called *Taijia* 太甲: "When Heaven makes calamities, one can still avoid them, but who makes his own calamities cannot survive". The received *Canon of Documents* (*Shangshu* 尚書) includes a chapter entitled "Taijia", and this passage is included in it, but the chapter is considered spurious.

41. Most notably by A. R. Radcliffe-Brown (1881–1955), *Structure and Function in Primitive Society: Essays and Addresses* (Glencoe, IL: Free Press, 1952), 157ff.; see also Robert F. Campany, "Xunzi and Durkheim as Theorists of Ritual Practice", in *Discourse and Practice*, Frank Reynolds & David Tracy (eds) (Albany, NY: SUNY Press, 1992), 197–231.

42. For enquiries into Xunzi's military thought, see, for example, Andrew Meyer & Andrew Wilson, "*Sunzi Bingfa* as History and Theory", *Strategic Logic and Political Rationality: Essays in Honor of Michael I. Handel*, Bradford A. Lee & Karl F. Walling (eds) (London: Frank Cass, 2003), 106ff.; Mark Edward Lewis, *Sanctioned Violence in Early China* (Albany, NY: SUNY Press, 1990), 66–7, 130–31; and Robert T. Oliver, *Communication and Culture in Ancient India and China* (Syracuse, NY: Syracuse University Press, 1971), 205ff. Geoffrey Lloyd & Nathan Sivin, *The Way and the Word: Science and Medicine in Early China and Greece* (New Haven, CT: Yale University Press, 2002), 66, write that the supposed debate is really "a form of entertainment for courtiers", a judgement influenced by the structure of the chapter (but no other evidence).

43. An authoritative statement of the motivation and methodology of the Doubting-Antiquity School can be found in the preface to *Gushi bian* 古史辨, by Gu Jiegang 顧頡剛 (1893–1980), translated as *The Autobiography of a*

Chinese Historian: Being the Preface to a Symposium on Ancient Chinese History (Ku shih pien), Arthur W. Hummel (trans.) (Leiden: Brill, 1931).

44. The point was evidently not recognized by Joseph Needham & Krzysztof Gawlikowski, "Chinese Literature on the Art of War", in *Science and Civilisation in China*, Joseph Needham *et al.* (eds) (Cambridge: Cambridge University Press, 1954–), vol. 6, 65, who referred to this chapter as Xunzi's own account of the debate.

45. Scholars disagree over Xunzi's dates. Knoblock, *Xunzi*, I, 1–35, argues for *c.*310–*c.*210 BCE.

46. The name Sun (i.e. instead of Xun) may have been used to avoid the taboo-name of Emperor Xuan of the Han 漢宣帝 (r. 76–48 BCE), who changed his personal name to Xun 詢 in 64 BCE (see the references in note 13, above). This suggestion is disputed – but if it is true, the consequence would have to be that someone had a hand in editing the "Yibing" chapter after 64 BCE.

47. Knoblock, *Xunzi*, II, 331 n.4.

48. Cf. Lewis, *Sanctioned Violence in Early China*, 116, 129ff., for discussions of this idea in the Warring States.

49. Cf. Goldin, *After Confucius*, 52–3.

50. Cf. William S.-Y. Wang, "Language in China: A Chapter in the History of Linguistics", *Journal of Chinese Linguistics* 17(2) (1989), 186ff.

51. For example, Graham writes that "the purpose of names ... is to show up clearly the similar and the different" (*Disputers of the Tao*, 263). Yes, but not for academic reasons; the purpose of names is to distinguish the similar and the different so that the sage king's subjects will understand his commands correctly.

52. For further discussion, see Goldin, *Rituals of the Way*, 144 n.35.

53. Because such paradoxes and their various proposed "solutions" seem straightforwardly reducible to logic problems familiar from Western philosophy, they have received an inordinate degree of attention over the last few decades, as Yuri Pines bemoans in *Envisioning Eternal Empire: Chinese Political Thought of the Warring States Era* (Honolulu, HI: University of Hawaii Press, 2009), 225 n.18. Even a representative bibliography would be impossible in the space of one note. The likeliest interpretation of the "white horse" paradox, from a historical point of view, is Christoph Harbsmeier, "The Mass Noun Hypothesis and the Part–Whole Analysis of the White Horse Dialogue", in *Chinese Texts and Philosophical Contexts*, Rosemont (ed.), 49–66.

54. I borrow this phrase from W. V. Quine, *The Ways of Paradox and Other Essays*, rev. edn (Cambridge, MA: Harvard University Press, 1976), 3.

55. See, for example, Graham, *Disputers of the Tao*, 176–83.

56. Hagen, *The Philosophy of Xunzi*, 59–84.

57. On the technical term *shi*, see Graham, *Later Mohist Logic, Ethics and Science*, 196–99.

58. Cf. Goldin, *Rituals of the Way*, 22ff.; and, more generally, Aaron Stalnaker,

"Aspects of Xunzi's Engagement with Early Daoism", *Philosophy East and West* 53(1) (2003), 87–129.

59. For an overview of scholarship on this term, see Sándor P. Szabó, "The Term *shenming* – Its Meaning in the Ancient Chinese Thought and in a Recently Discovered Manuscript", *Acta Orientalia* 56(2–4) (2003), 251–74.

60. For thoughts on whether this constitutes a mind–body problem, see my "A Mind-Body Problem in the *Zhuangzi*?" in *Hiding the World in the World: Uneven Discourses on the Zhuangzi*, Scott Cook (ed.) (Albany, NY: SUNY Press, 2003), 235–6.

5. Neo-Confucianism and Confucianism today

1. See, for example, Derk Bodde, "The State and Empire of Ch'in", in *The Cambridge History of China, vol. I: The Ch'in and Han Empires, 221 BC–AD 220*, Denis Twitchett & Michael Loewe (eds) (Cambridge: Cambridge University Press, 1986), 20. Bodde seems to assume that Westerners used this name because of the Qin unification, but this is improbable; the Qin empire was destroyed within fourteen years of its establishment, and most foreigners would never have known of its significance. Rather, it is more likely that the state of Qin, as the westernmost of the Warring States, was known through overland trade routes as the nearest point of entry to the Chinese world.

2. See especially Martin Kern, *The Stele Inscriptions of Ch'in Shih-huang: Text and Ritual in Early Chinese Imperial Representation* (New Haven, CT: American Oriental Society, 2000), 183–96.

3. The entire corpus has been translated by A. F. P. Hulsewé in *Remnants of Ch'in Law: An Annotated Translation of the Ch'in Legal and Administrative Rules of the 3rd century BC Discovered in Yün-meng Prefecture, Hu-pei Province, in 1975* (Leiden: Brill, 1985).

4. See, for example, Ulrich Lau, "The Scope of Private Jurisdiction in Early Imperial China: The Evidence of Newly Excavated Legal Documents", *Asiatische Studien* 59(1) (2005), 343ff.

5. See, for example, Michael Loewe, *Biographical Dictionary of the Qin, Former Han and Xin Periods (221 BC–AD 24)* (Leiden: Brill, 2000), 663.

6. See Nicolas Zufferey, "Debates on Filial Vengeance during the Han Dynasty", in *Dem Text ein Freund: Erkundungen des chinesischen Altertums: Robert H. Gassmann gewidmet*, Roland Altenburger *et al.* (eds) (Bern: Peter Lang, 2009), 77–90.

7. The discussion in A. F. P. Hulsewé, *Remnants of Han Law, vol. I: Introductory Studies and an Annotated Translation of Chapters 22 and 23 of the History of the Former Han Dynasty* (Leiden: Brill, 1955), 309–20, remains unsurpassed.

8. See Goldin, "Xunzi and Early Han Philosophy", 135ff.

9. The "Memorial on the Bone of the Buddha" is translated in Shih Shun Liu,

Chinese Classical Prose: The Eight Masters of the T'ang-Sung Period (Hong Kong: Chinese University Press, 1979), 44–9. The best study of Han Yu in English is Hartman, *Han Yü and the T'ang Search for Unity*. See also Peter K. Bol, *"This Culture of Ours": Intellectual Transitions in T'ang and Sung China* (Stanford, CA: Stanford University Press, 1992), 123–36.

10. For an informed reassessment of this term and its uses, see Peter K. Bol, *Neo-Confucianism in History* (Cambridge, MA: Harvard University Press, 2008), esp. 78–83.

11. Translated in Shih Shun Liu, *Chinese Classical Prose*, 140–43.

12. For the only book-length study of Ouyang Xiu in English, see James T. C. Liu, *Ou-yang Hsiu: An Eleventh-Century Neo-Confucianist* (Stanford, CA: Stanford University Press, 1967). See also Bol, *"This Culture of Ours"*, 177–201.

13. The term literally means "study of the Way", but is best left untranslated. It is taken from the ancient commentary to the *Great Learning*: "'As though chiseled, as though polished' – this is *daoxue*" 如切如磋, 道學也 (citing the famous line from Mao 55).

14. The fullest exposition in English of the Cheng brothers' philosophy is still A. C. Graham, *Two Chinese Philosophers: The Metaphysics of the Brothers Ch'eng* (London: Lund Humphries, 1958; reprinted, La Salle, IL: Open Court, 1992). See also Bol, *"This Culture of Ours"*, 300ff., for a discussion of Cheng Yi's philosophy in historical context.

15. In English, the most useful discussions are Bol, *Neo-Confucianism in History*, 163ff.; and Willard Peterson, "Another Look at *li* 理", *Bulletin of Sung-Yüan Studies* **18** (1986), 13–31. See also Wing-tsit Chan, "The Evolution of the Neo-Confucian Concept *li* as Principle", *Tsing Hua Journal of Chinese Studies* (new series) **4**(2) (1964), 123–47.

16. This definition, which went on to become standard, first arose in the context of a discussion by Xu Heng 許衡 (1209–81); see Huang Zongxi 黃宗羲 (1610–95) *et al.*, *Song Yuan xue an* 宋元學案 (*Guoxue jiben congshu* 國學基本叢書),22.128.

17. Cf. "Liu Yuancheng shoubian" 劉元承手編, *Henan Chengshi yishu* 河南程氏遺書, in *Er Cheng ji* 二程集, Wang Xiaoyu 王孝魚 (ed.), 2nd edn (Beijing: Zhonghua, 2004), 18.188.

18. "Ru Guan yulu" 入關語錄, *Henan Chengshi yishu, Er Cheng ji* 15.157; Graham (trans.), *Two Chinese Philosophers*, 9–10.

19. For an account of Zhu Xi's discussions with Lü Zuqian and others, see Hoyt Cleveland Tillman, *Confucian Discourse and Chu Hsi's Ascendancy* (Honolulu, HI: University of Hawaii Press, 1992).

20. Li Jingde, *Zhuzi yulei*, 9.156; Daniel K. Gardner (trans.), *Learning to Be a Sage: Selections from the* Conversations of Master Chu, Arranged Topically (Berkeley, CA: University of California Press, 1990), 125.

21. Li Jingde, *Zhuzi yulei*, 12.207; Gardner, *Learning to Be a Sage*, 169.

22. *Ibid.*, 42.

23. *Lu Jiuyuan ji* 陸九淵集, Zhong Zhe 鍾哲 (ed.) (Beijing: Zhonghua, 1980), 34.395.

24. Careful study of Zhu's and Lu's remarks on the value of reading reveals, as scholars have noted, that their respective positions were not so dissimilar. Lu also recognized the potential benefit of reading, and Zhu agreed that book learning was only a "secondary matter" for students. The real difference between the two thinkers lies on the metaphysical plane: whereas Zhu distinguishes between the reader's mind and the *li* of the text, for Lu the mind and *li* are equivalent. Zhu, therefore, urges reading as a method of *gewu*, of apprehending the principle of things external to the mind; for Lu, reading is a form of self-reflection. Cf. Edward T. Ch'ien, *Chiao Hung and the Restructuring of Neo-Confucianism in the Late Ming* (New York: Columbia University Press, 1986), 255ff.

25. Cf. "Those who learned in ancient times did it for themselves; those who learn today do it for others" (*Analects* 14.24).

26. Tu Wei-ming, *Way, Learning, and Politics: Essays on the Confucian Intellectual* (Albany, NY: SUNY Press, 1993), 83–4 (with romanization converted to *pinyin*).

27. "Ti Liang xiansheng Yunge" 題梁先生芸閣, in *Chen Xianzhang ji* 陳獻章集, Sun Tonghai 孫通海 (ed.) (Beijing: Zhonghua, 1987), 4.323; Jen Yu-wen (trans.), "Ch'en Hsien-chang's Philosophy of the Natural", in *Self and Society in Ming Thought*, W. Theodore de Bary (ed.) (New York: Columbia University Press, 1970), 80.

28. Max Weber, *The Religion of China: Confucianism and Taoism*, Hans H. Gerth (trans.) (New York: Macmillan, 1951), 163–4. One of the most sophisticated assessments of Weber is Thomas A. Metzger, *Escape from Predicament: Neo-Confucianism and China's Evolving Political Culture* (New York: Columbia University Press, 1976), 3ff. For an alternative point of view, see Wm. Theodore de Bary, "Confucian Education in Premodern East Asia", in *Confucian Traditions in East Asian Modernity: Moral Education and Economic Culture in Japan and the Four Mini-Dragons*, Tu Wei-ming (ed.) (Cambridge, MA: Harvard University Press, 1996), 21–37.

29. Talcott Parsons, *The Structure of Social Action*, 2nd edn (Glencoe, IL: Free Press, 1961), 549.

30. Weber, *The Religion of China*, 247–8.

31. Ezra F. Vogel, *The Four Little Dragons: The Spread of Industrialization in East Asia* (Cambridge, MA: Harvard University Press, 1991), 92ff. See also Tu Wei-ming's influential article, "A Confucian Perspective on the Rise of Industrial East Asia", in *Confucianism and the Modernization of China*, Silke Krieger and Rolf Trauzettel (eds) (Mainz: Hase & Koehler, 1991), 29–41.

32. See, for example, Jerome Ch'en, "The Chinese Communist Movement to 1927", in *The Cambridge History of China, vol. 12: Republican China 1912–1949, Part 1*, John K. Fairbank (ed.) (Cambridge: Cambridge University Press, 1983),

505–26, for a history of the beginnings of the CCP and Chen Duxiu's role in its establishment.

33. "Benzhi zui'an zhi dabian shu" 本誌罪案之答辯書, *Xin qingnian* **6**(1) (15 January 1919), 10 (where the words "democracy" and "science" appear in English in the original); Chow Tse-tsung, *The May Fourth Movement*, 59.

34. "*Ouyou xinying lu* jielu" 《歐遊心影錄》節錄, *Yinbingshi wenji dianjiao* 飲冰室文集點校, Wu Song吳松 *et al.* (eds) (Kunming: Yunnan jiaoyu, 2001), VI, 3481; Chow Tse-tsung, *The May Fourth Movement*, 328. See also Benjamin I. Schwartz, "Themes in Intellectual History: May Fourth and After", in Fairbank, *The Cambridge History of China*, 438–9; and Joseph R. Levenson, *Liang Ch'i-ch'ao and the Mind of Modern China*, 2nd edn (Berkeley, CA: University of California Press, 1967), 199–204, for assessments of this piece.

35. Cf. Guy S. Alitto, *The Last Confucian: Liang Shu-ming and the Chinese Dilemma of Modernity*, 2nd edn (Berkeley, CA: University of California Press, 1986), 112. Pankaj Mishra, "Sentimental Education in Shanghai", *New York Review of Books* (12 June 2008), wrongly asserts that Chinese intellectuals of this period disregarded Tagore.

36. For a similar view, see F. S. C. Northrop (1893–1992): "the East in its intuitionism and contemplation of things in their aesthetic immediacy, and the West in its pursuit of the theoretically known component, tended to brand the knowledge other than its own as illusory and evil" (*The Meeting of East and West: An Inquiry Concerning World Understanding* [New York: Macmillan, 1946], 454). Northrop's solution was that East and West can meet because "the two civilizations are shown to supplement and reinforce each other". Cf. Fred Setton, *An Introduction to the Philosophical Works of F. S. C. Northrop* (Lewiston, NY: Edwin Mellen, 1995), 55–71.

37. *Dong-Xi wenhua jiqi zhexue* (Beijing: Shangwu, 1999), 205; Alitto, *The Last Confucian*, 117, though he curiously omits the passages marked here in braces, for which I have inserted my own translations.

38. *Dong-Xi wenhua jiqi zhexue*, 213–14; Alitto, *The Last Confucian*, 122–3.

39. Carsun Chang, *The Development of Neo-Confucian Thought*, II, 476–7.

40. See especially Song Xianlin, "Reconstructing the Confucian Ideal in 1980s China: The 'Culture Craze' and New Confucianism", in *New Confucianism: A Critical Examination*, John Makeham (ed.) (Basingstoke: Palgrave Macmillan, 2003), 81–104.

41. Cf. John Makeham: "although *ruxue*-centered Chinese cultural nationalism is a movement, it is a movement largely restricted to academics" (*Lost Soul: "Confucianism" in Contemporary Chinese Academic Discourse* [Cambridge, MA: Harvard University Press, 2008], 16).

Appendix: Manhood in the *Analects*

1. See Chenyang Li, "The Confucian Concept of *Jen* and the Feminist Ethics of Care: A Comparative Study", in *The Sage and the Second Sex: Confucianism, Ethics, and Gender*, Chenyang Li (ed.) (La Salle, IL: Open Court, 2000), 23–42, and "Confucianism and Feminist Concerns: Overcoming the Confucian 'Gender Complex'", *Journal of Chinese Philosophy* 27(2) (2000), 187–99. See also James D. Sellmann & Sharon Rowe, "The Feminine in Confucius", *Asian Culture Quarterly* 26(3) (1998), 1–8.
2. See Herr, "Is Confucianism Compatible with Care Ethics?"; Julia Tao Lai Po-wah, "Two Perspectives of Care: Confucian *Ren* and Feminist Care", *Journal of Chinese Philosophy* 27(2) (2000), 215–40; and Joel J. Kupperman, "Feminism as Radical Confucianism: Self and Tradition", in *The Sage and the Second Sex*, Chenyang Li (ed.), 43–56.

   For more general explorations towards a rapprochement between Confucianism and feminism, see Li-hsiang Lisa Rosenlee, *Confucianism and Women: A Philosophical Interpretation* (Albany, NY: SUNY Press, 2006), esp. 149–60; Cecilia Wee, "Mencius, the Feminine Perspective, and Impartiality", *Asian Philosophy* 13(1) (2003), 3–13; Philip J. Ivanhoe, "Mengzi, Xunzi, and Modern Feminist Ethics", in *The Sage and the Second Sex*, Chenyang Li (ed.), 57–74; Eva Kit Wah Man, "Contemporary Feminist Body Theories and Mencius's Ideas of Body and Mind", *Journal of Chinese Philosophy* 27(2) (2000), 155–69; Sandra A. Wawrytko, "Kongzi as Feminist: Confucian Self-Cultivation in a Contemporary Context", *Journal of Chinese Philosophy* 27(2) (2000), 171–86; Terry Woo, "Confucianism and Feminism", in *Feminism and World Religions*, Arvind Sharma & Katherine K. Young (eds) (Albany, NY: SUNY Press, 1999), 110–47; Henry Rosemont, Jr, "Classical Confucian and Contemporary Feminist Perspectives on the Self: Some Parallels and Their Implications", in *Culture and Self: Philosophical and Religious Perspectives, East and West*, Douglas Allen (ed.) (Boulder, CO: Westview, 1997), 63–82; and Lik Kuen Tong, "The Way of Care: The Image of the Moral Guardian in Confucian Philosophy", in *New Essays in Chinese Philosophy*, Hsüeh-li Cheng (ed.) (New York: Peter Lang, 1997), 197–209.
3. Kam Louie, *Theorising Chinese Masculinity: Society and Gender in China* (Cambridge: Cambridge University Press, 2002), 42–57, offers an insightful study of Confucius as a model of manhood, but focuses on his reception in the twentieth century, not in his own society.
4. As quoted in Paul Ratchnevsky, *Genghis Khan: His Life and Legacy*, Thomas Nivison Haining (trans.) (Oxford: Blackwell, 1992), 153.

Guide to further reading

Ancient texts

Currently the best scholarly edition of the Confucian *Analects* is Huang Huaixin 黃懷信 *et al.*, *Lunyu huijiao jishi* 論語彙校集釋, 2 vols (Shanghai: Guji, 2008), which supersedes the edition that had been standard for decades: Cheng Shude 程樹德 (1877–1944), *Lunyu jishi* 論語集釋, 4 vols, Cheng Junying 程俊英 & Jiang Jianyuan 蔣見元 (eds) (Beijing: Zhonghua, 1990). A widely used edition for more casual reading is Qian Mu 錢穆 (1895–1990), *Lunyu xinjie* 論語新解 (Hong Kong: New Asia College, 1963), which is frequently reprinted in East Asia.

There is, unfortunately, no wholly satisfactory edition of the *Mencius*. The most frequently cited version is Jiao Xun 焦循 (1763–1820), *Mengzi zhengyi* 孟子正義, 2 vols, Shen Wenzhuo 沈文倬 (ed.) (Beijing: Zhonghua, 1987), but its scholastic orientation is not ideal for most modern study. Yang Bojun 楊伯峻, *Mengzi yizhu* 孟子譯注, 2 vols (Beijing: Zhonghua, 1960), is popular in East Asia, but not sufficiently inclusive for scholarly research.

For *Xunzi*, the most comprehensive edition is now Wang Tianhai 王天海, *Xunzi jiaoshi* 荀子校釋, 2 vols (Shanghai: Guji, 2005). Before, the standard edition had been Wang Xianqian 王先謙 (1842–1918), *Xunzi jijie* 荀子集解, 2 vols, Shen Xiaohuan 沈嘯寰 & Wang Xingxian 王星賢 (eds) (Beijing: Zhonghua, 1988).

Other canonical Confucian texts are collected in Ruan Yuan 阮元 (1764–1849), *Shisan jing zhushu fu jiaokan ji* 十三經注疏附校勘記 (Beijing: Zhonghua, [1815] 1980).

Translations

There are about two dozen complete translations of the *Analects* into Western languages. The best three, in my view, are *The Analects of Confucius*, Arthur Waley (1889–1966) (trans.) (London: Allen & Unwin, 1938); *Confucius: The Analects*, 2nd edn, D. C. Lau (trans.) (Hong Kong: Chinese University Press, 1992); and *The Analects of Confucius*, Edward Slingerland (trans.) (Indianapolis, IN: Hackett, 2003).

Mencius is less frequently translated than Confucius, but there are still some good choices: for example, *Mencius: A Bilingual Edition*, rev. edn, D. C. Lau (trans.) (Hong Kong: Chinese University Press, 2003) and *Mengzi: With Selections from Traditional Commentaries*, Bryan W. Van Norden (trans.) (Indianapolis, IN: Hackett, 2008).

There is only one complete translation of the *Xunzi* into English, and it is not always reliable: *Xunzi: A Translation and Study of the Complete Works*, 3 vols, John Knoblock (trans.) (Stanford, CA: Stanford University Press, 1988–94). Most of the important chapters are translated more loosely but also more fluidly in Burton Watson, *Xunzi: Basic Writings* (New York: Columbia University Press, 2003).

General surveys of Confucianism and ancient Chinese philosophy

The best overview of the intellectual world in which Confucianism developed is A. C. Graham, *Disputers of the Tao: Philosophical Argument in Ancient China* (La Salle, IL: Open Court, 1989). For a comprehensive study of the rise of written discourse in this period, see Mark Edward Lewis, *Writing and Authority in Early China* (Albany, NY: SUNY Press, 1999). Sociological enquiry is impeded by the dearth of sources, but the current state of archaeology is lucidly presented in Lothar von Falkenhausen, *Chinese Society in the Age of Confucius (1000–250 BC): The Archaeological Evidence* (Los Angeles, CA: Cotsen Institute of Archaeology, UCLA, 2006). Michael Loewe & Edward L. Shaughnessy (eds), *The Cambridge History of Ancient China: From the Origins of Civilization to 221 BC* (Cambridge: Cambridge University Press, 1999), remains helpful, but the pace of scholarship is not slow in this field, and eventually the book will have to be updated.

Good surveys of Confucianism are surprisingly hard to find. There are some useful papers in the following collections: David S. Nivison & Arthur F. Wright (eds), *Confucianism in Action* (Stanford, CA: Stanford University Press, 1959); Arthur F. Wright (ed.), *The Confucian Persuasion* (Stanford, CA: Stanford University Press, 1960); Arthur F. Wright & Denis Twitchett (eds), *Confucian Personalities* (Stanford, CA: Stanford University Press, 1962); Tu Weiming & Mary Evelyn Tucker (eds), *Confucian Spirituality*, 2 vols (New York: Crossroad, 2003–4); and Kwong-loi Shun & David B. Wong (eds), *Confucian Ethics: A Comparative Study of Self, Autonomy, and Community* (Cambridge: Cambridge University Press,

2004). (The first three, reflecting scholarly interest of the time, focus on post-classical Confucianism.) Nivison's own path-breaking researches have been edited by Bryan W. Van Norden as *The Ways of Confucianism: Investigations in Chinese Philosophy* (La Salle, IL: Open Court, 1996).

East Asian scholarship

Assuming primarily an English-speaking readership, I have mostly confined myself in this book to references in Western languages, but East Asian scholarship on Confucianism is enormous and cannot be neglected by any serious student. Representative overviews in Chinese include Huang Junjie 黃俊傑, *Dong Ya ruxue: Jingdian yu quanshi de bianzheng* 東亞儒學: 經典與詮釋的辯證 (Taipei: National Taiwan University Press, 2007); and Zhao Jihui 趙吉惠 *et al.*, *Zhongguo ruxue shi* 中國儒學史 (Zhengzhou: Zhongzhou guji, 1991). A handy recent collection of essays on the textual history of Confucian documents is Huang Huaixin & Li Jingming 李景明 (eds), *Rujia wenxian yanjiu* 儒家文獻研究 (Ji'nan: Qi-Lu, 2004). Important Japanese works include Kanaya Osamu 金谷治, *Kanaya Osamu Chūgoku shisō ronshū* 金谷治中國思想論集, 3 vols (Tokyo: Hirakawa, 1997), especially vol. 2; and Itano Chōhachi 板野長八, *Jukyō seiritsushi no kenkyū* 儒教成立史の研究 (Tokyo: Iwanami, 1995).

For Confucius and the *Analects*, Kimura Eiichi 木村英一, *Kōshi to Rongo* 孔子と論語 (Tokyo: Sōbunsha, 1971), remains seminal, especially for his account of the compilation of the *Analects*. Some Chinese works to be recommended are Qian Mu, *Kongzi zhuan* 孔子傳 (Beijing: Sanlian, 2002); and Cai Shangsi 蔡尚思 (ed.), *Shijia lun Kong* 十家論孔 (Shanghai: Renmin, 2006), a collection of extended excerpts from the works of ten famous Chinese scholars.

On Mencius and Xunzi: Wang Xingye 王興業 (ed.), *Mengzi yanjiu lunwenji* 孟子研究論文集 ([Ji'nan:] Shandong Daxue, 1984), which contains many essays by twentieth-century scholars; Cai Renhou 蔡仁厚, *Kong Meng Xun zhexue* 孔孟荀哲學 (Taipei: Xuesheng, 1984); Liao Mingchun 廖名春 (ed.), *Xunzi ershi jiang* 荀子二十講 (Beijing: Huaxia, 2009), another collection of previous scholarship; *idem, Xunzi xintan* 荀子新探 (Taipei: Wenjin, 1994); Wei Zhengtong 韋政通, *Xunzi yu gudai zhexue* 荀子與古代哲學 (Taipei: Shangwu, 1992); and Chen Daqi 陳大齊, *Xunzi xueshuo* 荀子學説 (Taipei: Zhongguo wenhua daxue, 1989).

1. Confucius and his disciples

For standard accounts of Confucius's life, see the references in Chapter 1, notes 13 and 14. Two influential interpretations of Confucius's philosophy that have not, in the main, been followed here are Herbert Fingarette, *Confucius: The Secular* as Sacred (New York: Harper & Row, 1972); and David L. Hall & Roger T. Ames, *Thinking Through Confucius* (Albany, NY: SUNY Press, 1987). The best historical study of commentary to the Confucian *Analects* is John Makeham, *Transmitters and Creators: Chinese Commentators and Commentaries on the* Analects (Cambridge, MA: Harvard University Press, 2003).

Finally, two recent collaborative volumes on the *Analects*: Bryan W. Van Norden (ed.), *Confucius and the* Analects: *New Essays* (Oxford: Oxford University Press, 2002); and David Jones (ed.), *Confucius Now: Contemporary Encounters with the* Analects (La Salle, IL: Open Court, 2008).

2. Interlude: *Great Learning* and *Canon of Filial Piety*

Filial piety, long neglected in Western scholarship, is the subject of a welcome new collaborative effort: Alan K. L. Chan & Sor-hoon Tan (eds), *Filial Piety in Chinese Thought and History* (London: Routledge Curzon, 2004). The work of Keith N. Knapp is valuable for its attention to the changing conceptions of filial piety over the course of Chinese history: for example, "The *Ru* Reinterpretation of *Xiao*", *Early China* 20 (1995), 195–222; and *Selfless Offspring: Filial Children and Social Order in Early Medieval China* (Honolulu, HI: University of Hawaii Press, 2005).

Great Learning is rarely discussed today except in the context of Neo-Confucianism, for which some standard references will be supplied below.

3. Mencius

The most authoritative book on Mencius is Kwong-loi Shun, *Mencius and Early Chinese Thought* (Stanford, CA: Stanford University Press, 1997). For a philosophically informed interpretation of Mencius as a great ancient exponent of virtue ethics, see Bryan W. Van Norden, *Virtue Ethics and Consequentialism in Early Chinese Philosophy* (Cambridge: Cambridge University Press, 2007), 199–314. Two recent collections of essays are Xiusheng Liu & Philip J. Ivanhoe (eds), *Essays on the Moral Philosophy of Mengzi* (Indianapolis, IN: Hackett, 2002); and Alan K. L. Chan (ed.), *Mencius: Contexts and Interpretations* (Honolulu, HI: University of Hawaii Press, 2002). The noted Western critic I. A. Richards (1893–1979) wrote a book about Mencius that was remarkably perceptive for its time: *Mencius on the Mind: Experiments in Multiple Definition* (New York: Harcourt, Brace, 1932).

4. Xunzi

For a book-length account of Xunzi's philosophy, I recommend my *Rituals of the Way: The Philosophy of Xunzi* (La Salle, IL: Open Court, 1999). T. C. Kline III

& Philip J. Ivanhoe (eds), *Virtue, Nature, and Moral Agency in the* Xunzi (Indianapolis, IN: Hackett, 2000), contains many important articles (most previously published elsewhere), including Eric Hutton's concise and insightful "Does Xunzi Have a Consistent Theory of Human Nature?" (220–36).

Aaron Stalnaker, *Overcoming Our Evil: Human Nature and Spiritual Exercises in Xunzi and Augustine* (Washington, DC: Georgetown University Press, 2006), is admirable for the author's deep understanding of both of the thinkers that he compares.

5. Neo-Confucianism and Confucianism today

In the twentieth century, the leading scholar of Neo-Confucianism in North America was Wing-tsit Chan, who compiled more works than can be listed here. Foremost among them is probably *A Source Book in Chinese Philosophy* (Princeton, NJ: Princeton University Press, 1963), which, despite its intrusive traditionalism, still contains the only available English translations of dozens of texts. Chan also wrote two respected books on the philosophy of Zhu Xi, namely *Chu Hsi: Life and Thought* (Hong Kong: Chinese University Press, 1987); and *Chu Hsi: New Studies* (Honolulu, HI: University of Hawaii Press, 1989). The most persuasive interpreter of Zhu Xi today is Daniel K. Gardner, for example, *Chu Hsi and the Ta-hsueh: Neo-Confucian Reflection on the Confucian Canon* (Cambridge, MA: Harvard University Press, 1986); *Learning to Be a Sage: Selections from the* Conversations of Master Chu, Arranged Topically (Berkeley, CA: University of California Press, 1990); and *Zhu Xi's Reading of the* Analects: *Canon, Commentary, and the Classical Tradition* (New York: Columbia University Press, 2003).

For the intellectual history of Neo-Confucianism, see the two books by Peter K. Bol: *"This Culture of Ours": Intellectual Transitions in T'ang and Sung China* (Stanford, CA: Stanford University Press, 1992); and *Neo-Confucianism in History* (Cambridge, MA: Harvard University Press, 2008). Robert P. Hymes and Conrad Schirokauer (eds), *Ordering the World: Approaches to State and Society in Sung Dynasty China* (Berkeley, CA: University of California Press, 1993), is an outstanding conference volume on Neo-Confucian political thought.

The best account of the contemporary "New Confucianism" movement is John Makeham, *Lost Soul: "Confucianism" in Contemporary Chinese Academic Discourse,* (Cambridge, MA: Harvard University Press, 2008). See also John Makeham (ed.), *New Confucianism: A Critical Examination* (Basingstoke: Palgrave Macmillan, 2003).

Bibliography

Alitto, G. S. 1986. *The Last Confucian: Liang Shu-ming and the Chinese Dilemma of Modernity*. 2nd edn. Berkeley, CA: University of California Press.

Ames, R. T. 1991. "The Mencian Conception of *Ren xing* 人性: Does It Mean 'Human Nature'?" In *Chinese Texts and Philosophical Contexts: Essays Dedicated to Angus C. Graham*, H. Rosemont Jr (ed.), 143–75. La Salle, IL: Open Court.

Ames, R. T. 2008a. "Paronomasia: A Confucian Way of Making Meaning". See Jones (2008), 37–48.

Ames, R. T. 2008b. "Whatever Happened to 'Wisdom'? Confucian Philosophy of Process and 'Human Becomings'". *Asia Major* (3rd series) 21(1): 45–68.

Bagley, R. W. 2004. "Anyang Writing and the Origin of the Chinese Writing System". In *The First Writing: Script Invention as History and Process*, S. D. Houston (ed.), 190–249. Cambridge: Cambridge University Press.

de Bary, W. T. 1996. "Confucian Education in Premodern East Asia". In *Confucian Traditions in East Asian Modernity: Moral Education and Economic Culture in Japan and the Four Mini-Dragons*, Tu Wei-ming (ed.), 21–37. Cambridge, MA: Harvard University Press.

Berling, J. 1985. "Self and Whole in Chuang Tzu". In *Individualism and Holism: Studies in Confucian and Taoist Values*, D. J. Munro (ed.), 101–20. Ann Arbor, MI: University of Michigan Center for Chinese Studies.

Bloom, I. 1985. "On the Matter of the Mind: The Metaphysical Basis of the Expanded Self". In *Individualism and Holism: Studies in Confucian and Taoist Values*, D. J. Munro (ed.), 293–330. Ann Arbor, MI: University of Michigan Center for Chinese Studies.

Bloom, I. 1994. "Mencian Arguments on Human Nature (*Jen-hsing*)". *Philosophy East and West* 44(1): 19–53.

Bodde, D. 1986. "The State and Empire of Ch'in". In *The Cambridge History of China, vol. I: The Ch'in and Han Empires, 221 BC–AD 220*, D. Twitchett & M. Loewe (eds), 21–102. Cambridge: Cambridge University Press.

Bol, P. K. 1992. *"This Culture of Ours": Intellectual Transitions in T'ang and Sung China*. Stanford, CA: Stanford University Press.

Bol, P. K. 2008. *Neo-Confucianism in History*. Cambridge, MA: Harvard University Press.

Boodberg, P. A. 1979. *Selected Works of Peter A. Boodberg*, A. P. Cohen (ed.). Berkeley, CA: University of California Press.

Brindley, E. F. 2010. *Individualism in Early China: Human Agency and the Self in Thought and Politics*. Honolulu, HI: University of Hawaii Press.

Brooks, E. B. & A. Taeko Brooks (trans.) 1998. *The Original Analects: Sayings of Confucius and His Successors*. New York: Columbia University Press.

Campany, R. F. 1992. "Xunzi and Durkheim as Theorists of Ritual Practice". In *Discourse and Practice*, F. Reynolds & D. Tracy (eds), 197–231. Albany, NY: SUNY Press.

Chan, A. K. L. 2002. "A Matter of Taste: *Qi* (Vital Energy) and the Tending of the Heart (*Xin*) in *Mencius* 2A.2". In *Mencius: Contexts and Interpretations*, A. K. L. Chan (ed.), 42–71. Honolulu, HI: University of Hawaii Press.

Chan, A. K. L. & Sor-hoon Tan (eds) 2004. *Filial Piety in Chinese Thought and History*. London: Routledge Curzon.

Chan Sin-wai 1984. *An Exposition of Benevolence: The Jen-hsüeh of T'an Ssu-t'ung*. Hong Kong: Chinese University Press.

Chan, Sin Yee 1999. "Disputes on the One Thread of *Chung-Shu*". *Journal of Chinese Philosophy* **26**(2): 165–86.

Chan, Wing-tsit 1964. "The Evolution of the Neo-Confucian Concept *li* as Principle". *Tsing Hua Journal of Chinese Studies* (new series) **4**(2): 123–47.

Chang, Carsun 1957–62. *The Development of Neo-Confucian Thought*, 2 vols. New York: Bookman.

Chang, Hao 1971. *Liang Ch'i-ch'ao and Intellectual Transition in China, 1890–1907*. Cambridge, MA: Harvard University Press.

Ch'en, J. 1983. "The Chinese Communist Movement to 1927". In *The Cambridge History of China, vol. 12: Republican China 1912–1949, Part 1*, J. K. Fairbank (ed.), 505–26. Cambridge: Cambridge University Press.

Chen Lai 2009. "'*Ru*': Xunzi's Thoughts on *ru* and Its Significance", Yan Xin (trans.). *Frontiers of Philosophy in China* **4**(2): 157–79.

Chen, Ning 1997. "The Concept of Fate in *Mencius*". *Philosophy East and West* **47**(4): 495–520.

Chen Xianzhang 陳獻章 1987. *Chen Xianzhang ji* 陳獻章集, Sun Tonghai 孫通海 (ed.). Beijing: Zhonghua.

Cheng Yi 程頤 and Cheng Hao 程顥 2004. *Er Cheng ji* 二程集, 2nd edn, Wang Xiaoyu 王孝魚 (ed.). Beijing: Zhonghua, 2004.

Ch'ien, E. T. 1986. *Chiao Hung and the Restructuring of Neo-Confucianism in the Late Ming*. New York: Columbia University Press.

Chow, Kai-wing 1994. *The Rise of Confucian Ritualism in Late Imperial China: Ethics, Classics, and Lineage Discourse*. Stanford, CA: Stanford University Press.

Chow Tse-tsung 1960a. "The Anti-Confucian Movement in Early Republican China". In *The Confucian Persuasion*, A. F. Wright (ed.), 288–312. Stanford, CA: Stanford University Press, 1960.

Chow Tse-tsung 1960b. *The May Fourth Movement: Intellectual Revolution in Modern China*. Cambridge, MA: Harvard University Press.

Cook, S. 1997. "Xun Zi on Ritual and Music". *Monumenta Serica* 45: 1–38.

Cook, S. 2000. "Consummate Artistry and Moral Virtuosity: The 'Wu xing' 五行 Essay and Its Aesthetic". *Chinese Literature: Essays, Articles, Reviews* 22: 113–46.

Creel, H. G. 1960. *Confucius and the Chinese Way*. New York: Harper & Row.

Creel, H. G. 1979. "Discussion of Professor Fingarette on Confucius". *Studies in Classical Chinese Thought*, H. Rosemont Jr & B. I. Schwartz (eds). *Journal of the American Academy of Religion* 47(3), Thematic Issue S: 407–15.

Csikszentmihalyi, M. 2001. "Confucius". In *The Rivers of Paradise: Moses, Buddha, Confucius, Jesus, and Muhammad as Religious Founders*, D. N. Freedman & M. J. McClymond (eds), 233–308. Grand Rapids, MI: Eerdmans.

Csikszentmihalyi, M. 2002. "Confucius and the *Analects* in the Hàn". See Van Norden (2002a), 134–62.

Cua, A. S. 2005. *Human Nature, Ritual, and History: Studies in Xunzi and Chinese Philosophy*. Washington, DC: Catholic University of America Press.

Defoort, C. 2008. "The Profit That Does Not Profit: Paradoxes with *li* in Early Chinese Texts". *Asia Major* (3rd series) 21(1): 153–81.

Ebrey, P. B. 1991. *Confucianism and Family Rituals in Imperial China: A Social History of Writing about Rites*. Princeton, NJ: Princeton University Press.

Eno, R. 2003. "The Background of the Kong Family of Lu and the Origins of Ruism". *Early China* 28: 1–41.

Esherick, J. W. & M. B. Rankin (eds) 1990. *Chinese Local Elites and Patterns of Dominance*. Berkeley, CA: University of California Press.

Fairbank, J. K. (ed.) 1983. *The Cambridge History of China, vol. 12: Republican China 1912–1949, Part 1*. Cambridge: Cambridge University Press.

Fei, Hsiao-tung 1953. *China's Gentry: Essays on Rural–Urban Relations*, M. P. Redfield (rev. & ed.). Chicago, IL: University of Chicago Press.

Fingarette, H. 1972. *Confucius: The Secular as Sacred*. New York: Harper & Row.

Fingarette, H. 1979. "Following the 'One Thread' of the *Analects*". *Studies in Classical Chinese Thought*, H. Rosemont Jr & B. I. Schwartz (eds). *Journal of the American Academy of Religion* 47(3), Thematic Issue S: 373–405.

Freedman, M. 1979. *The Study of Chinese Society*, G. W. Skinner (ed.). Stanford, CA: Stanford University Press.

Gale, E. M. 1931. *Discourses on Salt and Iron: A Debate on State Control of Commerce and Industry in Ancient China*. Sinica Leidensia 2. Leiden: Brill.

Gale, E. M. *et al.* 1934. "Discourses on Salt and Iron [*Yen T'ieh Lun*: Chaps. XX–XXVIII]". *Journal of the North China Branch of the Royal Asiatic Society* 65: 73–110.

Gardner, D. K. (trans.) 1990. *Learning to Be a Sage: Selections from the Conversations of Master Chu, Arranged Topically*. Berkeley, CA: University of California Press.

Gassmann, R. H. 2007. "Die Bezeichnung *jun-zi*: Ansätze zur Chun-qiu-zeitlichen Kontextualisierung und zur Bedeutungsbestimmung im *Lun Yu*". In *Zurück zur Freude: Studien zur chinesichen Literatur und Lebenswelt und ihrer Rezeption in Ost und West: Festschrift für Wolfgang Kubin*, M. Hermann & C. Schwermann (eds), 411–36. Sankt Augustin: Monumenta Serica, 2007.

Geaney, J. M. 1999. "A Critique of A.C. Graham's Reconstruction of the 'Neo-Mohist Canons'". *Journal of the American Oriental Society* 119(1): 1–11.

Gewirth, A. 1978. "The Golden Rule Rationalized". *Midwest Studies in Philosophy* 3: 133–47.

Gewirth, A. 1981. *Reason and Morality*. Chicago, IL: University of Chicago Press.

Goldin, P. R. 1999. *Rituals of the Way: The Philosophy of Xunzi*. La Salle, IL: Open Court.

Goldin, P. R. 2000. "Review of Roger T. Ames, ed., Wandering at Ease in the Zhuanzi". *Journal of the American Oriental Society* 120(3): 474–7.

Goldin, P. R. 2002. *The Culture of Sex in Ancient China*. Honolulu, HI: University of Hawaii Press.

Goldin, P. R. 2003a. "A Mind–Body Problem in the *Zhuangzi*?" In *Hiding the World in the World: Uneven Discourses on the Zhuangzi*, S. Cook (ed.), 226–47. Albany, NY: SUNY Press.

Goldin, P. R. 2003b. "Review of A. C. Graham, tr., *Chuang-tzu: The Inner Chapters*, and Harold D. Roth, *A Companion to Angus C. Graham's Chuang-tzu: The Inner Chapters*". *Early China* 28: 201–14.

Goldin, P. R. 2005a. *After Confucius: Studies in Early Chinese Philosophy*. Honolulu, HI: University of Hawaii Press, 2005.

Goldin, P. R. 2005b. "Response: Xunzi, Again". *Dao* 5(1): 204–6.

Goldin, P. R. 2005c. "The Theme of the Primacy of the Situation in Classical Chinese Philosophy and Rhetoric". *Asia Major* (3rd series) 18(2): 1–25.

Goldin, P. R. 2006. "Review of Alan A. K. Chan and Sor-hoon Tan, eds., *Filial Piety in Chinese Thought and History*". *Dao* 5(2): 371–5.

Goldin, P. R. 2007. "Xunzi and Early Han Philosophy". *Harvard Journal of Asiatic Studies* 67(1): 135–66.

Goldin, P. R. 2008. "Appeals to History in Early Chinese Philosophy and Rhetoric". *Journal of Chinese Philosophy* 35(1): 79–96.

Goldin, P. R. 2008. "When *Zhong* 忠 Does Not Mean 'Loyalty'". *Dao* 7(2): 165–74.

Goldin, P. R. 2009. "Hsiao Kung-chuan on Mencian Populism". In *Xiao Gongquan xueji* 蕭公權學記, Wang Rongzu 汪榮祖 & Huang Junjie 黃俊傑 (eds), 249–63. Taipei: National Taiwan University Press.

Graham, A. C. 1978. *Later Mohist Logic, Ethics and Science*. Hong Kong: Chinese University Press.

Graham, A. C. 1989. *Disputers of the Tao: Philosophical Argument in Ancient China*. La Salle, IL: Open Court.

Graham, A. C. 1990. *Studies in Chinese Philosophy and Philosophical Literature*. Albany, NY: SUNY Press.

Graham, A. C. 1958. *Two Chinese Philosophers: The Metaphysics of the Brothers Ch'eng*. London: Lund Humphries; reprinted, La Salle, IL: Open Court, 1992.

Hagen, K. 2006. *The Philosophy of Xunzi: A Reconstruction*. La Salle, IL: Open Court.

Hall, D. L. & R. T. Ames 1987. *Thinking Through Confucius*. Albany, NY: SUNY Press.

Hall, D. L. & R. T. Ames 1995. *Anticipating China: Thinking through the Narratives of Chinese and Western Culture*. Albany, NY: SUNY Press.

Han Yu 韓愈 1972. *Han Changli wenji jiaozhu* 韓昌黎文集校注, Ma Tongbo 馬通伯 (ed.). Beijing: Zhonghua.

Harbsmeier, C. 1991. "The Mass Noun Hypothesis and the Part–Whole Analysis of the White Horse Dialogue". In *Chinese Texts and Philosophical Contexts: Essays Dedicated to Angus C. Graham*, H. Rosemont Jr (ed.), 49–66. La Salle, IL: Open Court.

Hardy, G. 1999. *Worlds of Bronze and Bamboo: Sima Qian's Conquest of History*. New York: Columbia University Press.

Hartman, C. 1986. *Han Yü and the T'ang Search for Unity*. Princeton, NJ: Princeton University Press.

Hattori, U. 1936. "Confucius' Conviction of His Heavenly Mission", S. Elisséeff (trans.). *Harvard Journal of Asiatic Studies* 1(1): 96–108.

Herr, R. S. 2003. "Is Confucianism Compatible with Care Ethics? A Critique". *Philosophy East and West* 53(4): 471–89.

Holzman, D. 1998. "The Place of Filial Piety in Ancient China". *Journal of the American Oriental Society* 118(2): 185–99.

Hsiao, Harry Hsin-I 1978. "A Preliminary Interpretation of the Origin of the Concept of *hsiao* in the Shang Period". *Chinese Culture* 19(3): 5–20.

Hsiao, Harry Hsin-I 1979. "Concepts of *hsiao* in the *Classic of Poetry* and the *Classic of Documents*". *Journal of the Institute of Chinese Studies of the Chinese University of Hong Kong* 10(2): 425–43.

Hsiao, Kung-chuan 1975. *A Modern China and a New World: K'ang Yu-wei, Reformer and Utopian, 1858–1927*. Seattle, WA: University of Washington Press.

Hsu, Cho-yun 1965. *Ancient China in Transition: An Analysis of Social Mobility, 722–222 BC*. Stanford, CA: Stanford University Press..

Hu Zhihong 2008. "The Obscuration and Rediscovery of the Original Confucian Thought of Moral Politics: Deciphering Work on the Guodian, Shangbo and the Transmitted Versions of *Ziyi*", Huang Deyuan (trans.). *Frontiers of Philosophy in China* 3(4): 535–57.

Huang, Chun-chieh 2001. *Mencian Hermeneutics: A History of Interpretations in China*. New Brunswick, NJ: Transaction.

Huang Zongxi 黃宗羲 et al. *Song Yuan xue an* 宋元學案. Guoxue jiben congshu 國學基本叢書.

Hulsewé, A. F. P. 1955. *Remnants of Han Law*, vol. I: *Introductory Studies and an Annotated Translation of Chapters 22 and 23 of the History of the Former Han Dynasty*. Sinica Leidensia 9. Leiden: Brill.

Hulsewé A. F. P. (trans.) 1985. *Remnants of Ch'in Law: An Annotated Translation of the Ch'in Legal and Administrative Rules of the 3rd century BC Discovered in Yün-meng Prefecture, Hu-pei Province, in 1975*. Sinica Leidensia 17. Leiden: Brill.

Hummel, A. W. (trans.) 1931. *The Autobiography of a Chinese Historian: Being the Preface to a Symposium on Ancient Chinese History (Ku shih pien)*. Leiden: Brill.

Hutton, E. 2000. "Does Xunzi Have a Consistent Theory of Human Nature?" In *Virtue, Nature, and Moral Agency in the Xunzi*, T. C. Kline III & P. J. Ivanhoe (eds), 220–36. Indianapolis, IN: Hackett.

Ikeda Tomohisa 2004. "The Evolution of the Concept of Filial Piety (*xiao*) in the *Laozi*, the *Zhuangzi*, and the Guodian Bamboo Text *Yucong*". See Chan & Tan (2004), 12–28.

Ikezawa Masaru 池澤優 2002. *"Kō" shisō no shūkyōgakuteki kenkyū: Kodai Chūgoku ni okeru sosen sūhai no shisōteki hatten* 「孝」思想の宗教学的研究: 古代中国における祖先崇拝の思想的発展. Tokyo: Tōkyō Daigaku Shuppankai.

Ivanhoe, P. J. 2000. "Mengzi, Xunzi, and Modern Feminist Ethics". See Chenyang Li (2000a), 57–74.

Ivanhoe, P. J. 2002. "Confucian Self-Cultivation and Mengzi's Notion of Extension". In *Essays on the Moral Philosophy of Mengzi*, Xiusheng Liu & P. J. Ivanhoe (eds), 221–41. Indianapolis, IN: Hackett.

Ivanhoe, P. J. 2008. "The 'Golden Rule' in the *Analects*". See Jones (2008), 81–107.

Jen Yu-wen 1970. "Ch'en Hsien-chang's Philosophy of the Natural". In *Self and Society in Ming Thought*, W. T. de Bary (ed.), 53–92. New York: Columbia University Press.

Jensen, L. M. 1995. "Wise Man of the Wilds: Fatherlessness, Fertility, and the Mythic Exemplar, Kongzi". *Early China* 20: 407–37.

Jensen, L. M. 1997. *Manufacturing Confucianism: Chinese Traditions and Universal Civilization*. Durham, NC: Duke University Press.

Jensen, L. M. 2002. "The Genesis of Kongzi in Ancient Narrative: The Figurative as Historical". In *On Sacred Grounds: Culture, Society, Politics, and the Formation of the Cult of Confucius*, T. A. Wilson (ed.), 175–221. Cambridge, MA: Harvard University Press.

Jones, D. (ed.) 2008. *Confucius Now: Contemporary Encounters with the Analects*. La Salle, IL: Open Court.

Kaizuka, Shigeki 1956. *Confucius: His Life and Thought*, G. Bownas (trans.). London: Allen & Unwin.

Keightley, D. N. 2004. "The Making of the Ancestors: Late Shang Religion and Its Legacy". In *Religion and Chinese Society: A Centennial Conference of the École française d'Extrême-Orient*, J. Lagerwey (ed.), vol. 1, 3–63. Paris: École française d'Extrême-Orient.

Kern, M. 2000. *The Stele Inscriptions of Ch'in Shih-huang: Text and Ritual in Early Chinese Imperial Representation*. New Haven, CT: American Oriental Society.

Kern, M. 2005. "Quotation and the Confucian Canon in Early Chinese Manuscripts: The Case of 'Zi yi' (Black Robes)". *Asiatische Studien* 59(1): 293–332.

Kern, M. 2007. "The Performance of Writing in Western Zhou China". In *The Poetics of Grammar and the Metaphysics of Sound and Sign*, S. La Porta & D. Shulman (eds), 109–75. Leiden: Brill.

Kinney, A. B. 2004. *Representations of Childhood and Youth in Early China*. Stanford, CA: Stanford University Press.

Kline, T. C., III & P. J. Ivanhoe (eds) 2000. *Virtue, Nature, and Moral Agency in the* Xunzi. Indianapolis, IN: Hackett.

Knapp, K. N. 1995. "The *Ru* Reinterpretation of *Xiao*". *Early China* 20: 195–222.

Knapp, K. N. 2005. *Selfless Offspring: Filial Children and Social Order in Early Medieval China*. Honolulu, HI: University of Hawaii Press.

Knoblock, J. (trans.) 1988–94. *Xunzi: A Translation and Study of the Complete Works*, 3 vols. Stanford, CA: Stanford University Press.

Ko, D. 1994. *Teachers of the Inner Chambers: Women and Culture in Seventeenth-Century China*. Stanford, CA: Stanford University Press.

Ko, D. 2005. *Cinderella's Sisters: A Revisionist History of Footbinding*. Berkeley, CA: University of California Press.

Kohn, L. 2004. "Immortal Parents and Universal Kin: Family Values in Medieval Daoism". See Chan & Tan (2004), 91–109.

Kupperman, J. J. 2000. "Feminism as Radical Confucianism: Self and Tradition". See Chenyang Li (2000a), 43–56.

Lai, Karyn. "*Li* in the *Analects*: Training in Moral Competence and the Question of Flexibility". *Philosophy East and West* 56(1) (2006): 69–83.

Lau, D. C. (trans.) 1992. *Confucius: The Analects*, 2nd edn. Hong Kong: Chinese University Press.

Lau, D. C. (trans.) 2003. *Mencius: A Bilingual Edition*, rev. edn. Hong Kong: Chinese University Press.

Lau, U. 2005. "The Scope of Private Jurisdiction in Early Imperial China: The Evidence of Newly Excavated Legal Documents". *Asiatische Studien* 59(1): 333–52.

Lee, Janghee 2005. *Xunzi and Early Chinese Naturalism*. Albany, NY: SUNY Press.

Legge, J. (trans.) 1893–95. *The Chinese Classics*, 2nd edn, 5 vols. Oxford: Clarendon Press; reprinted, Taipei: SMC, 1991.

Levenson, J. R. 1959. *Liang Ch'i-ch'ao and the Mind of Modern China*, rev. edn. Cambridge, MA: Harvard University Press.

Levenson, J. R. 1967. *Liang Ch'i-ch'ao and the Mind of Modern China*, 2nd edn. Berkeley, CA: University of California Press.

Lévi, J. 2002. *Confucius*. Paris: Pygmalion/Gérard Watelet.

Levy, H. S. 1966. *Chinese Footbinding: The History of a Curious Erotic Custom*. New York: W. Rawls.

Lewis, M. E. 1990. *Sanctioned Violence in Early China*. Albany, NY: SUNY Press.

Lewis, M. E. 1999. *Writing and Authority in Early China*. Albany, NY: SUNY Press.

Li, Chenyang (ed.) 2000a. *The Sage and the Second Sex: Confucianism, Ethics, and Gender*. La Salle, IL: Open Court, 2000.

Li, Chenyang 2000b. "The Confucian Concept of *Jen* and the Feminist Ethics of Care: A Comparative Study". See Chenyang Li (2000a), 23–42.

Li, Chenyang 2000c. "Confucianism and Feminist Concerns: Overcoming the Confucian 'Gender Complex'". *Journal of Chinese Philosophy* 27(2): 187–99.

Li Jingde 黎靖德 1985. *Zhuzi yulei* 朱子語類, Wang Xingxian 王星賢 (ed.), 8 vols. Lixue congshu. Beijing: Zhonghua.

Liang Qichao 梁啟超 2001. *Yinbingshi wenji dianjiao* 飲冰室文集點校, Wu Song 吳松 *et al.* (ed.), 6 vols. Kunming: Yunnan jiaoyu.

Liang Shuming 梁漱溟 1999. *Dong-Xi wenhua jiqi zhexue* 東西文化及其哲學. Beijing: Shangwu.

Littlejohn, R. 2010. "Kongzi in the *Zhuangzi*". *Experimental Essays on Zhuangzi*, 2nd edn, V. H. Mair (ed.), 177–94. Dunedin, FL: Three Pines.

Liu, J. T. C. 1967. *Ou-yang Hsiu: An Eleventh-Century Neo-Confucianist*. Stanford, CA: Stanford University Press.

Liu, Shih Shun 1979. *Chinese Classical Prose: The Eight Masters of the T'ang-Sung Period*. Hong Kong: Chinese University Press.

Lloyd, G. & N. Sivin 2002. *The Way and the Word: Science and Medicine in Early China and Greece*. New Haven, CT: Yale University Press.

Lo, Yuet Keung 2004. "Filial Devotion for Women: A Buddhist Testimony from Third-Century China". See Chan & Tan (2004), 71–90.

Loewe, M. 2000. *Biographical Dictionary of the Qin, Former Han and Xin Periods (221 BC–AD 24)*. Leiden: Brill.

Louie, K. 1986. *Inheriting Tradition: Interpretations of the Classical Philosophers in Communist China, 1949–1966*. Oxford: Oxford University Press.

Louie, K. 2002. *Theorising Chinese Masculinity: Society and Gender in China*. Cambridge: Cambridge University Press.

Loy, Hui-chieh 2008. "*Analects* 13.3 and the Doctrine of 'Correcting Names'". See Jones (2008), 223–42.

Lu Jiuyuan 陸九淵 1980. *Lu Jiuyuan ji* 陸九淵集, Zhong Zhe 鍾哲 (ed.) Beijing: Zhonghua.

Ludwig, S. 2002. "Huan Kuan, Yantie lun: Die Debatte über Salz und Eisen", Erling von Mende (ed.). In *Vademecum zu dem Klassiker der chinesischen Wirtschaftsdebatten*, B. Schefold (ed.), 107–83. Düsseldorf: Handelsblatt.

Makeham, J. 1996. "The Formation of *Lunyu* as a Book". *Monumenta Serica* **44**: 1–24.

Makeham, J. 1998. "Between Chen and Cai: *Zhuangzi* and the *Analects*". In *Wandering at Ease in the* Zhuangzi, R. T. Ames (ed.), 75–100. Albany, NY: SUNY Press.

Makeham, J. 2003. *Transmitters and Creators: Chinese Commentators and Commentaries on* the Analects. Cambridge, MA: Harvard University Press.

Makeham, J. 2008. *Lost Soul: "Confucianism" in Contemporary Chinese Academic Discourse*. Cambridge, MA: Harvard University Press.

Man, Eva Kit Wah 2000. "Contemporary Feminist Body Theories and Mencius's Ideas of Body and Mind". *Journal of Chinese Philosophy* **27**(2): 155–69.

Metzger, T. A. 1976. *Escape from Predicament: Neo-Confucianism and China's Evolving Political Culture*. New York: Columbia University Press.

Meyer, A. & A. Wilson 2003. "*Sunzi Bingfa* as History and Theory". In *Strategic Logic and Political Rationality: Essays in Honor of Michael I. Handel*, B. A. Lee & K. F. Walling (eds), 99–118. London: Frank Cass.

Mishra, P. 2008. "Sentimental Education in Shanghai". *New York Review of Books* (12 June).

Møllgaard, E. 2007. *An Introduction to Daoist Thought: Action, Language, and Ethics in Zhuangzi*. London: Routledge.

Mou, Bo 2004. "A Reexamination of the Structure and Content of Confucius' Version of the Golden Rule". *Philosophy East and West* **54**(2): 218–48.

Mugitani Kunio 2004. "Filial Piety and 'Authentic Parents' in Religious Daoism". See Chan & Tan (2004), 110–21.

Mungello, D. E. 1985. *Curious Land: Jesuit Accommodation and the Origins of Sinology*. Wiesbaden: Franz Steiner; reprinted, Honolulu, HI: University of Hawaii Press, 1989.

Munro, D. J. (ed.) 1985. *Individualism and Holism: Studies in Confucian and Taoist Values*. Michigan Monographs in Chinese Studies 52. Ann Arbor, MI: University of Michigan Center for Chinese Studies.

Needham, J. & K. Gawlikowski 1954– . "Chinese Literature on the Art of War". In *Science and Civilisation in China*, Joseph Needham *et al.* (eds), V.6, 10–66. Cambridge: Cambridge University Press.

Needham, J. *et al.* (eds) 1954– . *Science and Civilisation in China*, 7 vols projected. Cambridge: Cambridge University Press.

Nivison, D. S. 1996. *The Ways of Confucianism: Investigations in Chinese Philosophy*, B. W. Van Norden (ed.). La Salle, IL: Open Court.

Northrop, F. S. C. 1946. *The Meeting of East and West: An Inquiry Concerning World Understanding*. New York: Macmillan.

Nussbaum, M. 2003. "Golden Rule Arguments: A Missing Thought?" In *The Moral*

Circle and the Self: Chinese and Western Approaches, Kim-chong Chong *et al.* (eds), 3–16. La Salle, IL: Open Court.

Nylan, M. 2001. *The Five "Confucian" Classics*. New Haven, CT: Yale University Press.

Nylan, M. with H. Huang 2008. "Mencius on Pleasure". In *Polishing the Chinese Mirror: Essays in Honor of Henry Rosemont, Jr*, M. Chandler & R. Littlejohn (eds), 244–69. New York: Global Scholarly Publications.

Nylan, M. & T. Wilson 2010. *Lives of Confucius: Civilization's Greatest Sage through the Ages*. New York: Doubleday.

Oliver, R. T. 1971. *Communication and Culture in Ancient India and China*. Syracuse, NY: Syracuse University Press.

Ommerborn, W. 2005. "Einflüsse des Menzius und seiner Theorie der Politik der Menschlichkeit (*renzheng*) in der Zeit vom 3. Jh. bis zum Ende der Tang-Zeit". *Archiv Orientální* **73**: 111–39.

Parsons, T. 1961. *The Structure of Social Action*, 2nd edn. Glencoe, IL: Free Press.

Peterson, W. 1986. "Another Look at *li* 理". *Bulletin of Sung-Yüan Studies* **18**: 13–31.

Pines, Y. 2002. "Lexical Changes in Zhanguo Texts". *Journal of the American Oriental Society* **122**(4): 691–705.

Pines, Y. 2005. "Disputers of Abdication: Zhanguo Egalitarianism and the Sovereign's Power". *T'oung Pao* **91**(4–5): 243–300.

Pines, Y. 2009. *Envisioning Eternal Empire: Chinese Political Thought of the Warring States Era*. Honolulu, HI: University of Hawaii Press.

Puett, M. J. 2002. *To Become a God: Cosmology, Sacrifice, and Self-Divinization in Early China*. Cambridge, MA: Harvard University Press.

Quine, W. V. 1976. *The Ways of Paradox and Other Essays*, rev. edn. Cambridge, MA: Harvard University Press.

Radcliffe-Brown, A. R. 1952. *Structure and Function in Primitive Society: Essays and Addresses*. Glencoe, IL: Free Press.

Rainey, L. 1998. "Mencius and His Vast, Overflowing *qi* (*haoran zhi qi*)". *Monumenta Serica* **46**: 91–104.

Ratchnevsky, P. 1992. *Genghis Khan: His Life and Legacy*, T. N. Haining (trans.). Oxford: Blackwell.

Roetz, H. 1998. *Konfuzius*, 2nd edn. Munich: C. H. Beck.

Rosemont, H., Jr 1997. "Classical Confucian and Contemporary Feminist Perspectives on the Self: Some Parallels and Their Implications". In *Culture and Self: Philosophical and Religious Perspectives, East and West*, D. Allen (ed.), 63–82. Boulder, CO: Westview.

Rosemont, H., Jr (ed.) 1991. *Chinese Texts and Philosophical Contexts: Essays Dedicated to Angus C. Graham*. La Salle, IL: Open Court.

Rosemont, H., Jr. & B. I. Schwartz (eds) 1979. *Studies in Classical Chinese Thought*. *Journal of the American Academy of Religion* **47**(3), Thematic Issue S.

Rosenlee, Li-hsiang Lisa 2006. *Confucianism and Women: A Philosophical Interpretation*. Albany, NY: SUNY Press.

Rule, P. A. 1986. *K'ung-tzu or Confucius? The Jesuit Interpretation of Confucianism*. Sydney: Allen & Unwin.

Russell, B. 1922. *The Problem of China*. London: Allen & Unwin.

Sanders, G. 2006. *Words Well Put: Visions of Poetic Competence in the Chinese Tradition*. Cambridge, MA: Harvard University Press.

Sato, Masayuki 2003. *The Confucian Quest for Order: The Origin and Formation of the Political Thought of Xun Zi*. Leiden: Brill.

Schwartz, B. I. 1983. "Themes in Intellectual History: May Fourth and After". In *The Cambridge History of China, vol. 12: Republican China 1912–1949, Part 1*, J. K. Fairbank (ed.), 406–50. Cambridge: Cambridge University Press.

Schwartz, B. I. 1985. *The World of Thought in Ancient China*. Cambridge, MA: Harvard University Press.

Sellmann, J. D. & S. Rowe 1998. "The Feminine in Confucius". *Asian Culture Quarterly* **26**(3): 1–8.

Setton, F. 1995. *An Introduction to the Philosophical Works of F. S. C. Northrop*. Lewiston, NY: Edwin Mellen.

Shaughnessy, E. L. 1991. *Sources of Western Zhou History: Inscribed Bronze Vessels*. Berkeley, CA: University of California Press.

Shun, Kwong-loi 1997. *Mencius and Early Chinese Thought*. Stanford, CA: Stanford University Press.

Shun, Kwong-loi 2002. "*Rén* 仁 and *Lǐ* 禮 in the *Analects*". See Van Norden (2002a), 53–72.

Sima Qian 司馬遷 1959. *Shiji* 史記, 10 vols. Beijing: Zhonghua.

Simson, W. J. 2006. *Die Geschichte der Aussprüche des Konfuzius (Lunyu)*. Bern: Peter Lang.

Slote, W. H. 1998. "Psychocultural Dynamics within the Confucian Family". In *Confucianism and the Family*, W. H. Slote & G. A. DeVos (eds), 37–51. Albany, NY: SUNY Press.

Sommer, M. H. 2000. *Sex, Law, and Society in Late Imperial China*. Stanford, CA: Stanford University Press.

Song Xianlin 2003. "Reconstructing the Confucian Ideal in 1980s China: The 'Culture Craze' and New Confucianism". In *New Confucianism: A Critical Examination*, J. Makeham (ed.), 81–104. Basingstoke: Palgrave Macmillan.

Stalnaker, A. 2003. "Aspects of Xunzi's Engagement with Early Daoism". *Philosophy East and West* **53**(1): 87–129.

Stalnaker, A. 2006. *Overcoming Our Evil: Human Nature and Spiritual Exercises in Xunzi and Augustine*. Washington, DC: Georgetown University Press.

Szabó, S. P. 2003. "The Term *shenming* – Its Meaning in the Ancient Chinese Thought and in a Recently Discovered Manuscript". *Acta Orientalia* **56**(2–4): 251–74.

Tan, Sor-hoon 2008. "Three Corners for One: Tradition and Creativity in the *Analects*". See Jones (2008), 59–77.

Tao Lai Po-wah, J. 2000. "Two Perspectives of Care: Confucian *Ren* and Feminist Care". *Journal of Chinese Philosophy* 27(2): 215–40.

Tillman, H. C. 1992. *Confucian Discourse and Chu Hsi's Ascendancy*. Honolulu, HI: University of Hawaii Press.

Tiwald, J, 2008. "A Right of Rebellion in the *Mengzi*?" *Dao* 7(3): 269–82.

Tong, Lik Kuen 1997. "The Way of Care: The Image of the Moral Guardian in Confucian Philosophy". In *New Essays in Chinese Philosophy*, Hsüeh-li Cheng (ed.), 197–209. New York: Peter Lang.

Tsuda Sōkichi 津田左右吉 1946. *Rongo to Kōshi no shisō* 論語と孔子の思想. Tokyo: Iwanami.

Tu Wei-ming 1989. *Centrality and Commonality: An Essay on Confucian Religiousness*. Albany, NY: SUNY Press.

Tu Wei-ming 1991. "A Confucian Perspective on the Rise of Industrial East Asia". In *Confucianism and the Modernization of China*, S. Krieger & R. Trauzettel (eds), 29–41. Mainz: Hase & Koehler.

Tu Wei-ming 1993. *Way, Learning, and Politics: Essays on the Confucian Intellectual*. Albany, NY: SUNY Press.

Van Norden, B. W. (ed.) 2002a. *Confucius and the* Analects: *New Essays*. Oxford: Oxford University Press.

Van Norden, B. W. 2002b. "Unweaving the 'One Thread' of *Analects* 4:15". See Van Norden (2002a), 216–36.

Van Norden, B. W. 2007. *Virtue Ethics and Consequentialism in Early Chinese Philosophy*. Cambridge: Cambridge University Press.

Vankeerberghen, G. 2005–6. "Choosing Balance: Weighing (*quan*) as a Metaphor for Action in Early Chinese Texts". *Early China* 30: 47–89.

Vogel, E. F. 1991. *The Four Little Dragons: The Spread of Industrialization in East Asia*. Cambridge, MA: Harvard University Press.

Waley, A. 1938. *The Analects of Confucius*. London: Allen & Unwin.

Wang, C. H. 1974. *The Bell and the Drum: Shih ching as Formulaic Poetry in an Oral Tradition*. Berkeley, CA: University of California Press.

Wang Ping 2000. *Aching for Beauty: Footbinding in China*. Minneapolis, MN: University of Minnesota Press; reprinted, New York: Anchor, 2002.

Wang Pu 王溥 1991. *Tang huiyao* 唐會要, 2 vols. Shanghai: Guji.

Wang, W. S.-Y. 1989. "Language in China: A Chapter in the History of Linguistics". *Journal of Chinese Linguistics* 17(2): 183–222.

Wang Xianqian 王先謙 1988. *Xunzi jijie* 荀子集解, Shen Xiaohuan 沈嘯寰 & Wang Xingxian 王星賢 (eds). Beijing: Zhonghua.

Wawrytko, S. A. 2000. "Kongzi as Feminist: Confucian Self-Cultivation in a Contemporary Context". *Journal of Chinese Philosophy* 27(2): 171–86.

Weber, M. 1951. *The Religion of China: Confucianism and Taoism*, H. H. Gerth (trans.). New York: Macmillan.

Wee, C. 2003. "Mencius, the Feminine Perspective, and Impartiality". *Asian Philosophy* 13(1): 3–13.

Wilde, O. 1966. *Complete Works of Oscar Wilde*. London: Collins.

Wilhelm, R. 1931. *Confucius and Confucianism*, G. H. Danton & A. P. Danton (trans.). New York: Harcourt Brace Jovanovich.

Woo, T. 1999. "Confucianism and Feminism". In *Feminism and World Religions*, A. Sharma & K. K. Young (eds), 110–47. Albany, NY: SUNY Press.

Wu Yu 吳虞 1922. *Wu Yu wenlu* 吳虞文錄, 2nd edn. Shanghai: Yadong tushuguan.

Wyatt, D. J. 1996. *The Recluse of Loyang: Shao Yung and the Moral Evolution of Early Sung Thought*. Honolulu, HI: University of Hawaii Press.

Zhu Xi 朱熹. *Chuci houyu* 楚辭後語. *Siku quanshu* 四庫全書.

Zhu Xi. 2001. *Sishu zhangju jizhu* 四書章句集注, Xu Deming 徐德明 (ed.). Shanghai: Guji.

Zufferey, N. 1995. "Pourquoi Wang Chong critique-t-il Confucius?" *Études Chinoises* **14**(1): 25–54.

Zufferey, N. 2003. *To the Origins of Confucianism: The Ru in Pre-Qin Times and During the Early Han Dynasty*. Bern: Peter Lang.

Zufferey, N. 2009. "Debates on Filial Vengeance during the Han Dynasty". In *Dem Text ein Freund: Erkundungen des chinesischen Altertums: Robert H. Gassmann gewidmet*, R. Altenburger *et al.* (eds), 77–90. Bern: Peter Lang.

Index of passages

Index